sea of sharks

A Sailor's World War II Survival Story

Elmer Renner
and Kenneth Birks

Naval Institute Press
Annapolis, Maryland

Naval Institute Press
291 Wood Road
Annapolis, MD 21402

Library of Congress Cataloging-in-Publication Data

Renner, Elmer, 1920–

   Sea of sharks : a sailor's World War II survival story / Elmer Renner and Kenneth Birks.

        p. cm.

   Includes bibliographical references.

   ISBN 1-59114-714-X

   1. Renner, Elmer, 1920– 2. YMS-472 (Ship) 3. Sailors—United States—Biography. 4. Shipwrecks—Pacific Ocean. 5. Survival after airplane accidents, shipwrecks, etc.—Pacific Ocean. I. Birks, Kenneth, 1924- II. Title.

   V63.R46A3 2004

   940.54'5973—dc22

                                                                            2004008407

At a time when the greatest war in the history of the world had ended, thousands of sailors and soldiers rejoiced and looked forward to their safe return to homes, families, and friends. Due to an act of nature, twenty-five crew members of YMS-472 never had this opportunity. It is in their memory that I dedicate this book.

Contents

Acknowledgments

After my retirement and prodding by my grandchildren, I wrote a short story of my survival of a typhoon at sea. Finished in 1986, I titled it *Survival*. Shortly after the typhoon and survival, while recovering in hospitals, I had made notes of the daily events on the raft in minute detail. Searching through records stored in boxes, I found my notes, now faded and worn, but legible, thus allowing me to portray each day's events accurately.

In 1993 a golfing friend of mine, Ken Birks, recommended that I consider writing a full-length book. Many hours were spent at Ken's home rewriting *Survival*. I express my thanks to Sylvia, Ken's wife, for her patience with Ken and me on all the Monday afternoons we spent writing the first draft. I always had a thought of writing a full-length book on the story, yet it was Ken who provided the impetus to do just that. I give him belated thanks for providing the push that was needed. I am truly sorry that Ken did not live to see the final version of *Sea of Sharks* in a published book. He passed away in April 2003.

I give thanks to my wife, Dorothy, and my family for their indulgence during the writing process. There were occasions when one or more of my four daughters thought I bordered on obsession, but everyone believed my project was worthwhile. Special thanks go to daughters "Always available" Sue, for her teaching skills, and Pat, for her literary knowledge, in guiding me in this effort. I also thank Jane and Barb, for their every encouragement to complete this project, and sons-in-law Ben, who provided emergency assistance in fixing computer glitches, Bruce, for the Sunday evening review of progress in the final writing, and Jim, who demonstrated the fruits of persistence.

SEA OF SHARKS

Introduction

In October 1944 I was assigned as the engineering officer to a skeleton crew of twelve seamen who were preparing YMS-472 for commissioning and wartime sea duty. Specially designed for minesweeping operations off coastal waters, she was constructed on an all-wood hull and was small for a U.S. Navy vessel, a bit over 130 feet in length with a complement of thirty-six men. Following commissioning and outfitting the ship was assigned to duty sweeping the entrance to New York harbor.

From the first YMS-472 was a hard luck ship. The duty in New York harbor should have been routine but it was not. On several occasions the sweeping gear became fouled in the ship's propellers, called screws, which required that one be repaired and both in time replaced. While tied at dock we were rammed by a submarine chaser. A few days after repairs, during a dense fog, we collided with a ship at anchor while crossing the crowded harbor. During our short months in New York we were in dry dock four times and had other repairs made at berth on three occasions. Our record was not enviable.

There was no accounting for it that I could see. Our captain was competent, the crew as able as any in the navy at that time, and the ship was well constructed. As sailors are subject to the whims of the sea and wind, and must rely on the condition of their vessel for survival, they tend to be a bit more superstitious than most. In our months in New York harbor a certain nagging doubt about our luck quietly crept into the talk of the men, although the officers attempted to make light of it.

In May 1945 the war in Europe came to an end and YMS-472 was assigned to duty with the Pacific Fleet. Along with one other minesweeper, we made our way south through the Panama Canal, then to Long Beach, California, where we were again outfitted. We sailed on to Hawaii, then Eniwetok, then Saipan, and finally Okinawa, where we joined the fleet.

During the voyage certain members of the crew began to note what they took as ominous coincidences. The ship with which we sailed from New York was YMS-454. Each vessel's numbers added up to thirteen. It took us thirteen days to reach Panama, then thirteen days to reach Long Beach. While at Long Beach we were united with two other ships to convoy to Hawaii: YMS-292 and YMS-436. Each vessel's numbers added up to thirteen. Our assigned course to Hawaii was 256; the course's numbers also added up to thirteen. Our time of arrival at Hawaii was scheduled to be 13 August and at Buckner Bay, Okinawa, on 13 September.

An uneasy feeling permeated our ship. The captain went so far as to request permission to be removed from the convoy. Permission was denied. En route to Okinawa that August we learned the war was over. With that news any thought that we were an unlucky crew aboard an ill-fated vessel vanished.

Our convoy anchored in Buckner Bay, Okinawa, to await final orders to sail on to Japan for duty clearing mines at the harbor of Sasebo. We were all understandably ecstatic at the unexpected ending of the war in the Pacific. Thoughts turned to the families waiting for us. My wife and I had been able to be together only a few months since I had completed naval cadet school at the U.S. Naval Academy in Annapolis in September 1943. I barely knew our fourteen-month-old daughter. Now, sooner than any of us had a right to expect, we would be reunited.

Members of the crew with sufficient time and duty quickly found themselves going home. They were replaced by others not so fortunate. We were all waiting our turn. Constant talk aboard ship was of family and of our future civilian life. The crew was kept busy with routine maintenance and the captain ran YMS-472 with a less firm, although no less competent, hand.

On the evening of 15 September the harbor was unnaturally calm, still as a municipal swimming pool in early morning. I went with others to our command ship to watch the 1945 movie *Rhapsody in Blue* starring Robert Alda, Joan Leslie, and Alexis Smith. I don't remember anything of the movie except the music, which was loud and clear. The night was especially beautiful, without the slightest stirring of air. The weather was so unusual we commented on it to one another on the shuttle boat as we returned to our vessel.

A few hours later, just after dawn, we were suddenly ordered to sea to ride out what later was described as one of the worst typhoons in recorded history. Although the warning caught us completely by surprise, we scrambled to secure the ship. YMS-472 was soon under way. The storm struck with incredible fury. Our small ship, designed for coastal waters, shuddered with the crash of each massive wave and threatened repeatedly to turn her bow against the 135 mile-per-hour winds. More than once YMS-472 rolled on her side beyond the specifications for the ship, but each time, ever so slowly, that fine, although unlucky, ship righted herself. Throughout the day and into that night the sea exacted a relentless toll as one system after another failed. In the darkness and amid the mountainous waves all of us in turn gave ourselves up as lost.

At 0100 on 17 September YMS-472 capsized in what proved to be the heart of the storm. Few of that wonderful young crew of thirty-one survived. This is the story of the handful who were cast adrift without food or water. Despite a betrayal, four rose, like Lazarus, from the dead.

Some names have been changed to spare the families from re-experiencing the tragedy and the loss of their loved ones during that fateful night of 16–17 September 1945.

Part One

THE
MAKURAZAKI
TYPHOON

ONE

Shipmates

If you are fortunate, you live your life in peace and tranquillity. If you are unlucky, there is a time when nothing is certain, when everything that has formed your existence vanishes, when your very survival hangs on the slightest whim of nature, on a variation in the wind, on the size and force of the next ocean wave.

If there is ever a time when you literally cling to life, it forever influences who you are. On the outside you struggle to remain the person you once were, the individual those you love depend upon, but within the recesses and dark corners of your soul, you have been altered, in a way so profound and fundamental, it takes a lifetime to face it.

Toward evening at my summer home on Lake Michigan I find myself drawn to the roof deck of the beach house. There I sit alone and wait quietly for sundown, my mind absent any thought. A single loon might skim the water's surface and from a distance I hear his forlorn call. A light breeze comes off the water and stirs a nearby poplar tree. The leaves are attached to the branches in such a way that when they are moved the branch itself remains motionless. The leaves flutter and flick and with the last of the day's sun shining on them they give the appearance of the lights of a distant city or of stars against the black sky on a clear night.

Activity on the lake slowly diminishes. As the sun moves lower to the horizon, there are fewer and fewer boats until finally the lake is at rest. It takes perhaps three minutes for the sun to completely disappear once it first touches the horizon, and I watch it faithfully until it is seemingly extinguished into the water. At that moment, with the expanse of water stretched before me, a profound depression descends and I am entirely consumed by thoughts of the approaching night and of the coming darkness. For a moment I am again a young man, fighting to survive a raging typhoon and then cast adrift in the vast Pacific.

I retreat from the beach house to the patio, drawing comfort from the stand of poplar trees, which shields me from the sight of the lake. The depression remains with me throughout the evening even though I am with family and friends and it is my final sensation as I later descend into a dreamless sleep. Each time I visit the lake I know this will happen, yet I always go to the beach house roof deck.

America had been in the Second World War for two years by 1943. During that time I had continued my studies in engineering at the University of Illinois. Like all eligible American men of my generation I had a draft number. The time when I would be called up was fast approaching. I wanted to complete my degree, if possible, as I had just two semesters remaining and this would have the added advantage of allowing me to enter the service as an officer.

I had served two years in the U.S. Army's ROTC program and knew from that experience that I did not want to go into the infantry. A U.S. Navy brochure announced the V-7 program, which would permit me to finish college before joining the war. I joined up. I graduated in February and was ordered to report to the U.S. Naval Academy at Annapolis, Maryland, in May to attend Officers Candidate School. I was commissioned an ensign 31 August 1943, then ordered to report to the Navy Diesel School at Penn State University.

When I was commissioned my fiancée, Dorothy, gave me a chain wristband with the inscription "Mizpah." I had attended grade and high school with Walter Truemper. Entering service before me, he served as a navigator on a bomber in the European theater. During a mission the pilot was seriously wounded and the copilot killed. Walter and another crewman took control of the plane and flew it until the rest of the crew bailed safely out. The pilot was too seriously injured to survive a parachute jump so Walter and another crewman attempted to land the bomber without success. He, the pilot, and the crewman were killed. Walter was awarded the Congressional Medal of Honor posthumously. A name associated with his plane had been "Mizpah," a biblical word from the book of Genesis. It means, "God be with you until we meet again." I was deeply moved by the gift and the band remained with me from that day on, although I was forced to remove it whenever I worked around engines.

Dorothy and I married and set up housekeeping for the next four months. I learned first to be a husband, then how to conduct myself as an officer, and finally what I needed to know about navy diesel engines. I completed my course of study in

January 1944 and was ordered to report to the canal zone in Panama for "duty afloat." The Panama Canal was vital to the American war effort because it allowed the timely transfer of warships between the two oceans as needed. It also saved weeks off the shipping times of vital resources from one coast to the other. Although no attack against its vulnerable locks was ever launched, the possibility was very real, and a portion of war resources was committed to keeping the vital link open.

Reluctant to leave my new wife, who was now pregnant, I knew this was a circumstance faced by many thousands at the time. There was nothing to be done but to get on with the war so I could come home and again live my life alongside my wife. I was young, in good health, and a newly commissioned officer. My country was at war, and I was understandably excited in anticipation of what lay ahead.

In Panama I served aboard an auxiliary minesweeper coastal *Brambling* (AMc-39), a small ship just ninety-six feet long, and I was able to spend most nights ashore. For a short time in April I was the officer-in-charge of another small vessel, *Parakeet*, a converted fishing boat. It was not an unpleasant way to spend a war. The most serious problem was the distance from my wife and worry over her pregnancy. In June I learned I was the proud father of a baby girl and distributed cigars to all my crew. During my routine fitness report I had listed my desire to attend the Mine Craft Training Center in Little Creek, Virginia, because this would allow me to see my family. My request was granted and in July I returned to the United States for my much-desired reunion with my wife and that wonderful first sight of my daughter.

The course of study lasted six weeks. There I met many of the men who were to form the nucleus for the crew of YMS-472. The U.S. Navy had brought certain members of the crew together at the school so they could begin the process of familiarization. There we studied equipment, minesweeping techniques, and the latest theories of minelaying and mine-sweeping methods.

My new skipper was Lt. (jg) Willard Blaser, a graduate of Ohio State University. About thirty years old, he had worked as an advertising executive in Cleveland, Ohio, before the war. The executive officer was Lt. (jg) Boyd Stauffer, who I didn't meet until later but he became a very close friend. Ens. Robert Hobart would serve as the electronics officer, and I was the engineering officer. Hobart was the only officer I outranked (by seniority), so I escaped the undesirable duty of being named commissary officer.

I was not so young and callow that I did not appreciate how very fortunate I had been. I had nearly been drafted out of college and in that event would by then have been serving in a combat infantry unit in either Europe or the Pacific. The scale of fighting had risen dramatically. With the landings at Normandy in Europe and Saipan in Asia, the casualty lists were enormous. Every death was the son of parents and possibly a husband of a young wife and maybe a father of small children. My duty until now had more in common with the peacetime navy than with the ominous war raging thousands of miles away, and I knew it.

In early September 1944, Blaser, myself, two petty officers from the engine room, and the nucleus of the deck crew were sent to Jacksonville, Florida, where our ship, YMS-472, was nearing completion at the Gibbs Gas Engine Company. My wife was able to join me for four days. I settled into a rooming house because this stationing was not on a navy base and lacked military housing.

Blaser proved to be an able captain who ran a good ship, in general. He was a handsome man of average height and build.

Although we were a small crew and the line between officer and enlisted men was not as especially rigid as it is in larger ships, he never seemed to warm to anyone, remaining a bit distant from all of us. We worked elbow to elbow for close to a year but I never felt close to him.

His wife had also joined him in Jacksonville, and they were staying at the same motel. The closest restaurant was down the street. Because Dorothy and I had no car we walked to it. It was a small thing but we ate our meals at the same time as the Blasers. He and his wife drove past my wife and I more than once yet he never offered us a ride. It struck a disappointing cord in me, although I suspect he didn't want to create the impression of a close relationship with any specific officer under his command. Blaser was not a bad man by any means, but the camaraderie that came naturally to the rest of us appeared to elude him. He was an able captain, however, and he repeatedly demonstrated his concern for our well being.

Prior to the war the Gibbs Company had serviced and installed marine diesel engines. Now it was manufacturing small ships for the U.S. Navy. It was a modest shipyard with just three vessels under construction. Ours was the farthest along and had already been launched. She was moored in a slip while being fitted out. My job was to report to the ship each morning and observe as the equipment and wiring were installed, the bunks assembled, and the final checks conducted. The civilian workers were very competent. Watching them work, I developed great confidence in the ship. The hull was made of Douglas fir planks two inches thick by six inches wide forming the outside skin, reinforced on the inside with one-inch planks. Ribs of white oak gave the hull additional support and shape.

In general, the vessel was well put together and I had no qualms about going to sea in her. Once under way she would have a crew of thirty-two men and four officers. Only eight had been to sea before, a not so unusual situation in those days of mass mobilization.

YMS-472 was our new home for the duration of the war. She was just 136 feet in length, 24 $\frac{1}{2}$ feet across at the beam, with a displacement of just 207 tons. She drew six feet of water and her superstructure rose thirty feet. At her normal cruising speed of twelve knots she could operate for eight days without refueling. It was going to be a tight fit for the crew of thirty-six. In such an environment lasting camaraderie tended to form more quickly than on the larger ships of the fleet.

During our time in Jacksonville the U.S. Navy was sending equipment to be installed or placed in the ship, including the armament, spare parts, tools, charts, navigation equipment, and galley implements. The materials were stored in a warehouse until ready for installation or to be taken aboard. We were all delighted to be united when the rest of the crew, which had been training at Little Creek, joined us. For the first time I met Boyd Stauffer, the senior officer with the group. We had not met earlier because Boyd had been with the deck crew during their training. There was warmth in his ever-present smile and the moment we shook hands I knew we would become fast friends.

The commissioning was scheduled to occur three days later. From that point forward U.S. Navy regulations required that an armed guard always be at the gangplank. The first in a series of incidents occurred. Slowly a pall was cast over the ship and her crew. The captain instructed Chief Gunners Mate Theodore Fits to go to the warehouse, locate a 45-caliber automatic handgun, clean it, and have it in readiness. It was left in a chicken wire enclosure as we continued with preparations for the commissioning exercise.

Early on the morning of 10 November the crew reported for duty with their gear and busied themselves moving into their new quarters. After they were settled an inspection was held to ensure that we were ready for commissioning. I was sent to the warehouse to retrieve the pistol but I couldn't find it. I searched repeatedly but the gun simply wasn't there. Fits helped me search but he could not find it. I informed the captain, who returned to the warehouse with me, and we searched once again.

The theft of a military weapon is a serious matter and has dire consequences for the culprit. Everyone was restricted to base, and the local FBI agent was summoned. I was ordered to accompany the agent as he searched the entire ship. He also went through the personal belongings of many of the men, some of whom I suggested. Ironically, a number of the men I suspected later turned out to be my closest friends, but at that time we did not know each other well. The search lasted a long time so the commissioning proceeded without me or the missing pistol. Fits was ordered to prepare another handgun.

Over the next few days we conducted trial runs, accompanied by civilian workers from the shipyard. Only minor problems developed and they were quickly fixed. On days that we remained at dock we transferred the last of the equipment onboard. We were now fully a part of the U.S. Navy fleet and I believe all of us felt a sense of pride in that. Stauffer received word at this time of his promotion to lieutenant junior grade and was roundly congratulated. The unpleasantness over the stolen handgun was forgotten.

While we were at Jacksonville a hurricane struck the east coast of Florida. The hurricane's eye came ashore some distance south of us so we did not experience the full force of the storm. We were warned that morning of the approaching gale so we had time to prepare. I was in a warehouse with the crew and witnessed the storm through a window. It grew dark as if it were night, and we were unable to see across the St. Johns River. Debris flew helterskelter; trees bent to the powerful wind howling outside. We commented with incredulity when some unexpected object flew past. The building shook, but there was never any question of it coming apart. Nor did we experience the slightest sense of danger. Still, the storm greatly impressed me with its power.

We were ordered to Charleston, South Carolina, to pick up our ammunition. Once onboard and again under way we testfired our deck guns and dropped several depth charges. In late November we were ordered to the Mine Craft Training School at Little Creek, Virginia. While there we completed our shakedown cruise, tested the ship at various speeds, and tried out the sonar, electronic equipment, and the moored mine cables. We put the YMS-472 and her gear through the paces. We also practiced man overboard and abandon ship procedures.

Safety was always a paramount concern. In the highly unlikely event that we were ever sunk we carried three flotation devices. A dinghy, located amidships immediately behind the superstructure, was used as a runabout in harbor. If necessary it could hold six to eight men. On each side of the superstructure a raft, designed to carry ten to twelve men, was latched. Survival supplies were fixed to the wooden lattice bottom on each raft. Doing the arithmetic, I realized that if all three devices were filled to overflow capacity there was just enough room for the entire crew. I commented to Stauffer that the arrangement seemed dangerously inadequate.

Off Little Creek we learned to sweep with our gear, practiced damage control, simulated runs on friendly submarines, fired our deck gun, and prepared ourselves for our role with the fleet. I was satisfied that we worked well together as a crew and knew our business. During this time I received word of my promotion to lieutenant junior grade. At the small celebration we received word that a destroyer had gone down during a hurricane. You cannot be a sailor long without learning respect for the power of the ocean. For a few moments my thoughts dwelled on what it would be like to be at sea amid high winds and waves, then to be sunk and at the mercy of the storm. I pushed the thoughts away because they aren't the kind any sailor wishes to keep.

I shared very tight quarters with Boyd Stauffer, so cramped only one of us was able to dress at a time. As I anticipated, we quickly become good friends. At five feet nine inches he was much shorter than I was. We both came from working class families. Like me he had also worked his way through college, in his case as a "soda jerk" at the campus pharmacy. In fact, he'd married the boss's daughter, Elizabeth, who was living with her parents in Philadelphia. They had a son named Andy.

Boyd and I were fiercely competitive. We never played a game without making a modest, although significant, bet. Rummy became our card game of choice and we maintained a running count of the score, which too often left me on the short end. Stauffer was responsible for scheduling the recreational activities of the crew and we routinely discussed various activities that might be of interest. We believed it was important that serving aboard our ship should be more than endless routine.

We were a tight crew. With the exception of Blaser, the line between officer and enlisted man was blurred. I personally could see no reason to maintain the kind of distance required in the big ships and was joined in this approach to camaraderie by both Hobart and Stauffer. Hobart was the youngest, fresh out of college and officer training. He had just been commissioned an ensign and YMS-472 was his first assignment. From central Indiana, he stood five feet ten inches, with a slender build and a baby face. He had been a radio buff all his life. At home he had operated a ham radio station and was devoted to radio equipment of all kinds. He was not athletically inclined and did not participate in any of the sports with the crew. More than any of us he loved to stay onboard and spend time playing with the radio. He was by nature a quiet young man, always willing to take someone else's watch, always cooperative. Although a large number of the crew engaged in less worthy activities ashore after we reached New York City, when on liberty Hobart visited museums, saw the tourist sites, or hung out at radio stores to view and test the latest equipment. His only vice, if you could call it that, was his love of cards. The navy had that effect on most of us.

On 3 December there was a short ceremony during which our mess cook, Harold Perry, was awarded the Purple Heart. He had served during the Normandy invasion and sustained injuries while sweeping the landing zone for mines while under fire. Perry was no more than twenty years old, slim, and perhaps five feet six inches in height. He was unassuming, eager to perform any task assigned. Raised by his single mother, a less common occurrence in those days, I knew his life had to have been hard.

I decided to spend Christmas Day taking in a round of golf. Bill Ash and Bill Harrison, two men I was getting to know and like more all the time, joined me along with another member of the crew. Harrison's first name was Herbert but he went by Bill. Well liked, he was of medium build and height. He always had a smile and was full of ideas. I knew he had leadership capabilities. Ash, on the other hand, was a very quiet person. He was maybe five feet eleven inches and slender. Ash and Harrison were each married and they often went on liberty together.

On 31 December 1944 we were ordered to Frontier Base Tompkinsville, Staten Island, New York, for minesweeping duty at the port of New York, the busiest port in the world at that time. We arrived off the harbor on New Year's Day and an air of excitement remained in the harbor from the celebration the night before. Entering was complicated because of wartime precautions. We expressed some concern as to whether or not we could manage to reach our berth without incident, but we succeeded.

There were seven other minesweepers stationed at the port. The practice was for us to work in teams of two or four. We took station about thirty miles out from the harbor. We swept four hours in one direction, turned, and repeated the procedure in the opposite direction but on a new path. On occasion we would do this for twenty-four hours at a stretch but most often we put into the U.S. Coast Guard base at Sandy Hook for the night. After seven days we returned to our regular berth for two or three days before going out to sea again. We worked in conjunction with a number of the ships but most often our partner ship was YMS-454.

One of our gunner's mates, Fred Gildore, had a chip on his shoulder. He was constantly either picking fights with the crew or joining one already started, often inciting those arguing to become violent. If our ship had a "bad apple," Gildore was it. Stauffer and I often discussed how we should handle him, because we feared one of the situations could get out of hand and become dangerous. That nearly happened when one of his combatants was ready to use a knife on him.

Niles McQueen, an electrician's mate, was a rough, hard spoken man from Louisiana where his mom ran a bar. Although not as combative as Gildore he was quick tempered and a know-it-all. He often acted on impulse. Worse, in my opinion, he was a loner who always looked out for himself. In such a small ship our great need was for team players and McQueen was anything but that. Of our two troublemakers, however, Gildore was the worst. Stauffer and I often discussed how to improve the situation because the pair hurt morale but we were never able to come up with a lasting solution. Otherwise, our ship had a very fine crew.

The purpose of a minesweeper is to detect and destroy mines. Mines can be laid in many ways but the most likely was for a German U-boat to sneak in close, then quietly digorge the mines at the entrance to the harbor or in its immediate shipping lanes. A mine could sink or cripple any ship unlucky enough to strike or pass over it. Although the war against the U-boats was going well by this time, the New York harbor was always vulnerable to mines. The navy was constantly alert and both the harbor and the approaches had to be swept continuously.

There were three kinds of mines. All were laid in shallow water. The YMS class of ships was designed as a coastal vessel for this purpose. The YMS was not designed to face the heavy seas and violent storms of the Atlantic and Pacific.

Contact mines, which were tethered by a cable to the ocean floor, had contact points bristling from them. The mine floated just below the surface of the water. When a ship struck the mine it was detonated. Magnetic mines were placed directly on the ocean floor, typically at the approach channels to a harbor. These were exploded by the magnetic field created from the metal hull and machinery of a ship under way. For that reason minesweepers are built of wood. Magnetic mines could be programmed to detonate with the passage of the first ship or could be programmed for a number of ships to pass before exploding, thus trapping the first several ships in the channel. Acoustic mine were detonated by the distinctive vibrations of a ship's engine.

YMS-472 was equipped with the most modern equipment in existence at the time. Two steel sweep cables, used alone or as a pair, were used for moored mines. A single electrical cable was used for magnetic mines. It was much larger in diameter than the steel cables and it was hollow to give it buoyancy. These three cables were wrapped on large reels mounted on the stern of the ship. On the bow was an air hammer that mimicked the engine sound of a large ship. Dropped into the water, it was used to explode acoustic mines.

The steel cables were run straight out the back of the ship for a distance of about three hundred feet. Because of special rigging attached to them, the cables then made a right angle turn and extended out two hundred feet on either side of the ship. We could sweep an area four hundred feet across at any one time. When the steel cables came in contact with the tethering cable of a mine, an explosive cutter attached at spaced intervals on the steel sweep cable would be triggered to detonate and sever the tethering cable, releasing the mine to float to the surface. Men were on watch to spot when this happened. They fired a machine gun at the mine until it exploded.

When we were sweeping for magnetic mines we extended the single electronic cable out five hundred feet directly to our stern. It was fitted with two electrode tips that protruded below the cable some distance apart. We alternated the polarity between these two tips and established a magnetic field that mimicked the kind for which the mine was set. When we passed close enough to such a mine the field would cause it to explode. We often swept for magnetic mines paired with another ship because we could cover a greater area by setting up a magnetic field between the ships' two cables and coordinating the polarity reversal.

The air hammer was attached to the end of a boom located on the bow of the ship. The boom could be lowered in the water when sweeping for mines or raised out of the water and secured in its raised position when out of service. The pivot joint for the boom structure, which straddled the bow, was located just above the water line. When lowered it extended some ten feet into the water. Compressed air was piped to the hammer mechanism that set up a pounding action against a drum producing vibrations comparable to that of a ship's engine. The noise produced was louder than that of a ship. When these vibrations were detected by an acoustic mine it exploded a safe distance ahead of us.

We had repeatedly practiced all the routines needed to properly operate the complicated equipment. None of the officers or crew had any concern about our ability to do our job. This demonstrated how little we understood the complexity of our function in actual operation.

At 0530 the morning of 7 January 1945 we proceeded to the area of the Ambrose Lightship, anchored on the seaward end of the marked channel into New York harbor. It was a very cold, dreary day with poor visibility caused by persistent fog. We were to sweep in tandem with YMS-454. We arrived on station just at daybreak and both ships began preparations to stream their magnetic cables.

This is a fairly complicated procedure and the captain assumed command of the vessel from the bridge to oversee it personally. Boyd Stauffer was on the stern with the deck crew.

I had no direct involvement, so I stood on the main deck to observe as the deck crew went about their duties. Instructions as to the cable, ship's speed, and direction, were relayed from the captain through the appropriate personnel until they reached the individual or individuals that actually carried out the task. Each step involved a number of crewmen and everyone had to do what was required for the process to work. If anyone misunderstood or misinterpreted an order, or carried out the wrong instruction, the consequences could be significant, costly, and even dangerous. This was the essential reason why we had to act as a team and why we had to trust one another.

The deck crew was going about preparations as they had dozens of times before. One of the men said, "Let's see how many mines we can pick up today." The area was under such a blanket of security and swept so continuously that finding a mine was quite rare. Although equipped and trained to sweep for mines and destroy them, finding one was dangerous work. A seaman who had taken part in the Italian invasion answered, "I'd just as soon have none. I don't need any more stars on my ribbons."

When they were ready Stauffer said, "Prepare to stream cable for sweeping." Blaser gave the order to proceed one-third ahead. Upon hearing the order the quartermaster on the bridge repeated it to Seaman Third Class Lester Talley who was manning the annunciator. He turned the handle and rang up, "One-third ahead," which the crew in the engine room read and returned the signal. Once on the proper heading Blaser gave the order, "Stream gear!"

As each one-hundred-foot interval went out Stauffer called it up to the captain. At four hundred feet all was well and Blaser gave the order, "Two-thirds ahead!" The orders were repeated aloud as required. Even though Talley said, "Ahead," he unintentionally set the annunciator at two-thirds astern, which meant the screws were suddenly turning to pull the ship backward, into the cable!

The deck crew members working on the fantail were now preparing to secure the cable for normal minesweeping duties as they had done many times before in practice. Before that was accomplished, however, it was obvious something was very wrong. The ship was no longer making headway. Instead, she was moving in the opposite direction. "What the hell's going on?" Stauffer shouted to the captain. "We're going backward!" I hurried down to lend a hand.

Blaser ordered, "Stop engines!" He then rushed from the bridge toward the fantail. Stauffer and I stared down into the water as we waited for the captain. "Shit," Boyd said, "I'll bet we're caught on one of the screws." We briefly discussed turning the screw the opposite direction in the hope the cable would come free but decided it was more likely to make the situation worse.

Blaser hurriedly made his way from the bridge to the stern of the ship. Approaching Stauffer, he said, "What the hell's going on? Why can't we stream the damn cable?" Then in a louder voice he repeated, "What the hell's going on?"

Stauffer shrugged his shoulders. In his disarming and friendly manner he said, "I don't know. We were about to secure the cable when I noticed we were making stern way. Apparently we backed up on the cable and I think it may be tangled on a screw. Why were we backing up?"

Blaser said we weren't supposed to be. Stauffer commented that perhaps the situation could still be salvaged. He gave the order to retrieve the cable. The cable's winch slowly started winding the long cable in. After about twenty feet were onboard the cable tightened and the winch groaned to a stall. The cable was definitely caught on something.

Two engines, each with a screw, drove the ship. A rudder was mounted on the hull directly behind each screw to steer the ship. There was nothing else for the cable to catch on. The rudders were turned and found to be free. Blaser and Stauffer spoke, then decided to start one of the engines to see if that was the screw on which the cable was caught. The port engine was engaged to slow forward and at once the cable on deck drew taut. The engine was stopped. To our great relief the starboard screw turned without a problem.

We had now been bobbing on the sea for some five minutes. During this time our sister ship, YMS-454, had successfully prepared to start sweeping operations without a noticeable problem. As we looked about it became clear we were in the middle of the only sea-lane leading into the harbor. We advised YMS-454 we were experiencing problems and notified base about what had happened. We requested permission to return to base after we retrieved the cable because it would be necessary to check the ship and equipment for damage. Overhearing the transmission, and because two ships were required to sweep for magnetic mines, our sister ship also requested permission to head to base. She was advised to stand by in the event we required assistance.

On the stern deck we considered what to do. We couldn't use the winch to bring the cable in. The sea was very rough and we didn't want to risk putting crewmen out in the dinghy. If we cut the cable loose there was no assurance it wouldn't just remain wrapped around our screw, and if it did float free there would be five hundred feet of cable drifting in the world's busiest sea-lane. We decided to bring the cable in from the opposite end.

Moving at a slow speed with our one engine and screw we turned into a circle to come up on the far end of the cable. From a distance we resembled a puppy chasing its own tail. Our concern was that the movement of the ship might start pulling the end of the cable along before we reached it. It looked as if we were going to make it, then with just a few yards to go the end of the cable moved away from us. There were moans all around.

We tried bursts of speed with no success. At the same distance the cable moved away from us. We tried sneaking up on it, then circling around the other direction. The same result—no luck! Then we stopped and threw a line repeatedly across the end of the cable but every time we pulled it back our line failed to catch.

The crew of YMS-454 watched us with what we could only assume was considerable humor. They were full of advice, all broadcast over the open airways. The various ships entering the harbor were soon aware of our plight and they too chipped in with bright ideas. As we circled repeatedly in search of our tail they took to calling us "Rover." Thinking back on it I've decided that the ship was engineered to prevent us from running over our own cable so we were never going to be able to catch it.

Blaser returned to the bridge. He approached Talley and asked, "What the hell did you ring up on the annunciator when I asked for two-thirds ahead?"

Talley replied, "Two-thirds ahead, sir."

"Well, damn it, there's something wrong. Get the log out."

He then radioed for permission to proceed on one engine to quieter waters at Sandy Hook. We thought that we'd be able to safely launch our dinghy there. We received permission. YMS-454 was told to head back to her berth. As she passed she blinked a parting message for our eyes only. YMS-454 would return with dog food so we could continue chasing our tail for as long as necessary. They also thanked us for their unexpected liberty.

En route to Sandy Hook, with time to settle the issue, the captain shouted, "Renner, get the engine room logs and get up here on the bridge!"

"Yes, sir," I answered and went below to retrieve them.

When I reached the bridge, Talley, who'd been manning the annunciator, was blaming the engine room for misinterpreting his command. Blaser demanded to know what kind of engine room I was running. I told him it was a good one. I'd brought Talley's counterpart, Ian Frye, from the engine room up with me. Talley insisted he'd given the right instruction. Frye said the order he'd received was for two-thirds astern, not forward. Although not yet twenty, Frye was married and was a steady member of the crew. He stayed out of the petty squabbling every small vessel has, and was extremely reliable. His word meant a great deal and what he said is what the log showed.

Talley was less mature than Frye and was the ship's practical jokester, not always showing the best of judgment in his pranks. He persisted in claiming he'd made no error until the captain realized that if the annunciator had been set one way and the engine room had done something else, an automatic alarm would have sounded. Talley had clearly made a major mistake.

The captain settled the question of disciplinary action. Talley was so low in rank there was no way to lower him. Someone with more experience was assigned to man the annunciator. The only good news from the experience was that no hard feelings, always a source of concern on a small ship, developed between the bridge crew and the engine room crew.

We reached the calmer waters of Sandy Hook at noon. More attempts to circle after the end of the cable were unsuccessful. When we nearly damaged our one good screw on a buoy, Blaser ordered the dinghy launched. The men were soon back with the cable. Now the real work began.

The magnetic cable was four to five inches in diameter and weighed more than ten pounds per foot. The only way to bring it aboard was by hand. We had no place to string the cable except all about the open deck. Everyone chipped in and after three hours we had four hundred feet of cable onboard. We were ready to head back to port using the ship's one engine.

It wasn't a pleasant trip. This had been one of our first real days on duty and we'd messed up. In addition, one of the most important pieces of our equipment was ruined and strewn all over the deck for everyone to see. We had just one operating engine, which made the ship difficult to steer. Everyone in the harbor knew what had happened. Most of all, we were certain dire consequences were going to come of this. We crept in just after dark, all of us dead tired.

By now the crew of YMS-454 was returning from their unexpected liberty, full of beer and jovial goodwill for us. Arriving two at a time, as if they were boarding the Ark, they asked how it happened. We'd tell the story, then the pair would thank us for their liberty and leave laughing. The next pair would arrive. This went on for hours.

Blaser was ordered to make a full report at 0800 the next morning. Possibly because we were all so new no official action was taken. A navy diver arrived at noon to inspect for damage and make the repair. It took three hours to free the cable. Unfortunately, but not surprisingly, the screw was heavily damaged. This meant we had to go into dry dock, but first all the ammunition and depth charges had to be safely removed from our ship. The morning we left our berth YMS-454 signaled us again, this time with a much appreciated, "Safe voyage." There proved to be no damage other than a mangled screw, so after just five days we were once more afloat. We retrieved our ammunition and returned to our berth. YMS-454 signaled, "Welcome back to the war."

Our new, and improved, magnetic cable was waiting for us aboard a barge. It took an hour to hook it up and then carefully wind it aboard. When this was done the entire crew broke into a cheer. We were operational again. When we successfully deployed our cable the crew cheered again as if we'd just sunk a U-boat. We performed two tours of nine days each sweeping without incident, much to our relief. It had been a shaky start but we were now a part of the war effort.

TWO

Thirteens

Very early on the morning of 22 January 1945 YMS-472 headed back out to sea, this time to resume minesweeping duties with YMS-454. It was an especially cold and inhospitable day with a heavy fog limiting visibility. Ensign Hobart was scheduled for the watch but because of the thick fog Captain Blaser took over while the ship maneuvered through the channel.

The vessels in the shipping lane were sounding their horns to alert everyone else where they were to avoid collisions. The sound was recurrent and in the murky conditions only added to the confusion. To remain in the channel we had to spot each buoy in turn. They were nearly impossible to find, because we couldn't see more than thirty feet ahead. Bells rang from each buoy and we had to listen very carefully to hear them. Still, we had radar to help with locating the buoys so the ship made steady, if slow, progress. As we approached the seaward end, Blaser returned the bridge watch to Hobart.

Three hours out, just as we passed the Ambrose Lightship, I felt a dull thud ripple along the length of our ship. At once a vibration began, indicating to me that one of our screws had been damaged. Neither the watch nor Hobart had seen anything, but it was obvious we'd struck an object in the water.

Blaser was summoned and was convinced we'd struck one of the buoys although the men on watch told him that was impossible because we were past the lightship and had reached an area where there were no buoys. After some discussion it was agreed we had most likely had the bad luck to collide with a partially submerged log. It happened to every ship at one time or another. We just couldn't understand why it had to happen to us so soon after our last trouble.

The captain resumed the bridge watch. Whatever the cause, at least one screw had certainly been damaged so it was not possible to complete our sweeping duties. Blaser radioed Tompkinsville for permission to return to base. YMS-454 tried to get approval to return with us, anticipating more liberty I knew, but she was told to continue her mission and work with the other vessels already sweeping. Now it was our turn to wish them well, tongue in cheek.

As we turned back for the harbor the fog immediately thickened. The buoys were spaced about one mile apart and we were reduced to listening for them. Having only one screw in operating condition, our ability to maneuver was limited, so radar was essential in these atrocious conditions. As we neared the turn for Sandy Hook, Blaser decided to put in to the U.S. Coast Guard base until the fog lifted.

This meant leaving the marked channel. The buoys for our new course were much smaller and it developed that our radar couldn't pick them up. They also lacked both lights and bells. With the dense fog we were all but blind. It wasn't long before our remaining good screw struck something. With a sinking heart I felt another dull thud and a now familiar kind of vibration pass through the ship.

Blaser ordered the engine stopped while we apprised our situation and used radar to determine our exact location. We were still some distance from the base in Sandy Hook so he finally decided it was safer to return to the main channel and resume the course to our regular base. Once under way there was clearly a problem with the remaining screw because the vibration continued. The ship was unable to proceed faster than one-third speed, which was about three knots. Now crawling, YMS-472 was a dangerous target for any other ship in the channel, any of which would surely be going faster than three knots.

It was slow, tedious work spotting the buoys. The going became especially treacherous when we left the marked channel and crawled through the many ships at anchor to reach our pier at Tompkinsville late that afternoon without further incident. Blaser went ashore and filed his report. Back onboard he called a meeting of the officers.

Blaser was angry and I could understand his frustration with having to once again explain our dilemma to the base commander. Nothing that had taken place was really anyone's fault but we still felt badly. Two incidents had taken place that day, each of them serious enough to disable the ship. Neither could be taken lightly. We just couldn't understand why so many unfortunate incidents were happening to us so quickly. Every ship had trouble, but not like this. We were also anticipating the hard work ahead in again preparing the ship for dry dock.

Mid-morning the next day the same diver arrived to inspect the damage. He cracked a few jokes because it was just twenty-six days since he'd last checked out YMS-472. Ten minutes after entering the water he was back to report that one screw was ruined beyond repair while the other was so seriously damaged it would require a complete overhaul. This was disheartening news.

Every ship carried as many spares as possible. Other parts were stored ashore and followed the vessel from home base to home base. We'd already used one of our two spare screws, and it wasn't likely it had yet been replaced. The extra screw we needed had to be taken from another ship's spare. We again off-loaded the ammunition and depth charges, a tedious chore, then made our way back to McWilliams Shipyard on the northern tip of Staten Island. As luck had it we were assigned the same dock and civilian crew who had repaired our ship before. There was plenty of good-natured hazing about our becoming such good customers, although by now we were a bit thin skinned about it all. Five days later we retrieved our ammunition and reported yet again for duty.

The next morning, 7 February, YMS-472 was sent to resume regular minesweeping duties, accompanied by YMS-454. We experienced more incidents but nothing as serious as our earlier ones. Every few days we put in at Sandy Hook for refueling and reprovisioning.

My fellow officers and I were becoming concerned about morale. Because we'd had so many tough incidents and had become the brunt of humor, morale among our crew was generally pretty poor. If we didn't do something, we feared that our ship was in danger of turning into a hard luck ship. Stauffer said he'd heard the small U.S. Coast Guard base at Sandy Point had a basketball court so he suggested a basketball game with the crew of YMS-454. Blaser agreed, as did the skipper of our sister ship.

We put in, gathered volunteers and spectators from our crew, then went off laughing to the court. The court turned out to be for the use of enlisted personnel only. I was one of the taller guys onboard and although not the best player, my shipmates wanted me to play. Stauffer thought about it a moment then told them we'd be right back. Aboard ship we changed into enlisted clothes and then returned to play a number of games against the other crew. We were the better players and our prowess on the court lifted ship morale considerably. Blaser knew what Stauffer and I were doing but never said a word to stop it. We didn't give a moment's thought to the risk we were taking as officers impersonating enlisted men. There would have been serious trouble if we had been found out. Luckily no one gave us away. We played many basketball games with YMS-454's crew and later with crews from other minesweepers our ship was partnered with.

There were other positive developments as well. Every week we were on duty the crew was becoming more of a team although the traditional squabbling between the engine room gang, who saw to the engineering needs of the ship, and the deck crew was always present. Harrison, constantly on the move, talking endlessly, had installed a hotplate below to brew coffee and I spent more time in the engine room drinking coffee than I did in the officers' wardroom. Eventually Harrison was cooking ham and egg breakfasts, complete with orange juice. The engineering team became very close knit.

The men of YMS-472 represented a broad cross-section of America. Many had abilities that came to light only in certain circumstances. Freeman Hetzer, for example, was assigned to us while we were stationed in New York. He was from Chicago and single. Perhaps six feet in height, and lanky, he was not more than nineteen years old, like so many of the crew. He had brown hair with blue eyes and was always bursting with new ideas.

He wasn't the only one. When we were berthed at Tompkinsville, members of the crew wanted to be able to use the ship's dinghy for getting about the harbor. Unfortunately, oars propelled the dinghy, and no one liked that. YMS-472 was not authorized a motor for the dinghy so we were stuck rowing until one of the crew came up with a plan using the ship's portable gasoline-powered fire-fighting pump. He adapted the pump and installed it on the dinghy. He rigged it to suck the water from the bow and jet it out the stern. Now we had a jet-powered dinghy that we used to cruise all around the harbor.

At about this time I attended a going away dinner for a friend whose ship was being transferred to the Pacific. We all had more to drink than we should have. As a result, I was pretty rocky the next morning when we were ordered back to our minesweeping duties. During my watch I unsuccessfully fought seasickness, something I suffered from almost every first day at sea. All too frequently I found myself throwing up over the side. On one of my excursions I smelled very hot fumes coming from the exhaust port on the side of the ship. Aboard such a small vessel every sailor quickly becomes accustomed to the routine sounds, vibrations, and smells on the ship. Anything out of the ordinary roused immediate interest. These fumes were much too hot. I notified the engine crew and they reported back that the port side engine was running close to red.

The engine had to be shut down and once again our sweeping duties with YMS-454 would be abandoned. Given our history this was not something I wanted to do but I had no choice. I issued the appropriate orders and sent for the captain. After learning of our difficulty, YMS-454 should have signaled us discreetly. Instead, the broadcast was in the open, "Permission granted, Rover."

Blaser arrived on the bridge in an agitated state. The men who had performed the inspection reported that a large diameter rope had washed overboard and was apparently wrapped around the port screw. We received permission to return to base. YMS-454 was ordered to remain on station and to continue sweeping in conjunction with the other ships in the area. When we docked, the captain delivered his report. Although he had escaped a "chewing out" until now, this time he was lectured for allowing the deck crew to be so careless in stowing a line.

Back onboard ship Blaser fixed the blame on Cox'n Mate Gerald Doring because he had overall responsibility for securing the deck. A soft-spoken, unflappable crewman, Doring never involved himself in the almost endless bickering between the deck crew and the engineering gang. He was only a bit taller than average but very powerfully built. His presence as the "big" man under the basket contributed to our basketball success. It was a shame he took the heat, but that's how the navy works.

The same diver made quick work and cut away the rope in half an hour. Anticipating at least five days of liberty, the crew groaned when he reported he could see no damage. "Too bad, boys," he said with a grin. We were immediately ordered back to duty. YMS-454's crew was in its usual jovial mood and signaled they were glad to see us out of the kennel. They said they'd believe we were truly ready for duty when they actually saw our cable strung out behind us. None of us had a sense of humor about our situation any longer. We just wanted to be a normal ship having the normal range of experiences.

The next two weeks passed routinely. At regular nightly intervals we put into the base at Sandy Hook for refueling and a basketball game, followed by a few beers. We continued dominating in play against our sister ship and that helped take the sting out of events. Once a week we were back at base, which meant liberty for half the crew.

We were all becoming more comfortable with one another, with just a few exceptions. One night when I had duty I heard a commotion in the crew's mess. I wasn't paying much attention to it when suddenly the door to the wardroom opened and in staggered the steward's mate, highly agitated and covered with what looked like blood. Chasing him was Talley, a butcher knife raised over his head as if to strike him. I shot up out of my chair, scared out of my wits. The pair scuffled. Upon seeing my reaction, they broke into laughter. The blood was ketchup. They were just having a good time at my expense. There were other good-natured pranks but none were more frightening than this one.

Because we were in dry dock so often, YMS-472 was the best known of the minesweepers in the harbor. In time, the kidding became good-natured. When Bill Harrison won fifty thousand Camel cigarettes on a radio quiz show, we became very popular indeed because everyone hoped to get their hands on some of the booty. Other ships stopped addressing us as "Rover" and began calling us "Smokey."

Harrison and I had become quite good friends and we often spent liberty in New York together. He was always energetic, cheerful, and a fine companion. I was constructing a scale model of our ship, and because there was no kit to assemble I was always visiting anywhere I could to find wood or anything else that would help. Harrison often came along to help out.

Ian Frye, known simply as Frye, was another good friend. He was big but not fat. He had large hands and feet. Affable and highly likable, he was looking to get ahead and was studying for promotion to motor machinist mate first class. He asked for my help with his studies and I was glad to give it. Bright and rock solid, I wished I had ten just like Frye.

On the morning of 9 February YMS-472 was tied to the pier along with two other ships ahead of us. The engine room crew was busy taking on fuel while the mess section stowed provisions. The deck crew was busy with the endless chore of chipping and repainting. The two berths to our stern were empty. As I gazed out across the open water I spotted a small submarine chaser turn toward one of the open berths.

Common practice is to watch any new ship dock to judge the competence of its captain. I could see the vessel intended to tie up behind us. It seemed to me the ship was coming in a bit too fast but I wasn't too concerned because I didn't know her characteristics. What seemed fast to me might have actually been a crawl to the oncoming ship. As the ship drew nearer there was no lessening of her speed, in fact, during those last few feet she seemed to accelerate—straight into us.

Even a submarine chaser is a ship with a great deal of mass. All of this was happening in slow motion but with substantial momentum. There was the sickening crunch of wood and a dull shudder throughout the length of YMS-472. It was unbelievable. There could be no question of fault because our ship was tied to a berth! Once the submarine chaser backed off I sent a team to inspect the damage, which proved to be not quite as extensive as I had feared. Later I went aboard the chaser and learned that her screws had not reversed, as they should have. Instead of acting as a brake, the nonreversed screws caused the ship to accelerate. YMS-472 returned to dry dock for repairs, then she was ordered back on duty.

Not quite two weeks later we were returning from five days of duty at sea when we were quickly engulfed in the worst fog I had ever experienced. We were reduced to crawling in the water, relying almost entirely on radar to locate the essential buoys as we proceeded up the channel. We had a lookout stationed at the bow to call buoys out as they were spotted. Blaser was in command of the ship at the time. Radar wasn't effective with objects really close to us, and in that same range the lookout was blind as well. It was both nerve-racking and dangerous. We turned from the marked channel to head for our berth at Tompkinsville.

To get to our berth, we had to leave the main channel and cross through a large area where ships were anchored at random, often in a large cluster, all waiting to be off-loaded or loaded at a pier. Wending our way through this mass had to be done very carefully. We proceeded as slowly as we possibly could. Shortly after making our turn from the channel a large freighter loomed directly in front of us, appearing literally out of nowhere.

"All engines back full!" Blaser shouted. Our ship slowed and we watched in apprehension until our ship finally stopped just five feet short of the other vessel. We breathed a sigh of relief as we slowly eased back and began increasing the distance between us. Suddenly, we all felt a slight shudder, then heard the sickening crunch made by splitting wood. We had backed into an anchored Liberty ship that we had passed earlier but hadn't seen due to the fog.

The damage was exactly where repairs had just been done. An inspection indicated the most serious damage was above the water line so the ship was taking on very little water. Fortunately, our steering mechanism had escaped damage. We proceeded to our berth at a greatly reduced speed and arrived thirty minutes later. The captain prepared the now all too familiar report and went off to see the base commander. We were ordered into dry dock for five days once again.

This turn of events was disheartening. The night before we were ordered to return to duty, I was officer of the day and as the only officer onboard greeted the crew as they returned from liberty. At about 2200, Robert Hicks, one of the cox'n mates, knocked on my door. From Alabama, he was no more than twenty years old. He was short and burly with a pronounced nose and a rough-and-tumble look. He had always been quiet, even a little shy. He'd been on liberty with Martin Engler and Art Shockley, a helmsman, but wanted to talk to me before turning in. It was common following liberty for crewmen to report complaints or incidents so that is what I was expecting. I asked Hicks to sit down. I'd been gluing a part to my ship's model.

"What's wrong, Bob?" I asked. "Someone get in a fight?"

He shook his head. "No, but when we were walking from the ferry to the dock we got to talking about all the problems we've been having. You know the cable, the rope getting caught, getting rammed in the stern, the missing gun at commissioning, backing into the Liberty ship. Well, we got to thinking if there was something wrong with us, like maybe we're jinxed or something."

"I don't think so." This was the first time I had heard anyone talk about us being a jinxed ship.

He went on. "Some of the guys said the ships numbers added up to thirteen. We're not superstitious or anything but we thought you should know what the guys are talking about."

"Do you know who else is talking like this?" I asked.

"No, but maybe Engler does."

"Get Engler. Let's talk to him."

Engler arrived. Shockley, who stood in silence, accompanied him. I said, "What's this I hear about the ship's numbers adding up to thirteen?"

Engler, a signalman and a fairly lighthearted guy, seemed embarrassed by the question. "Oh, nothing. I just heard a few guys from the bridge crew talking about our numbers and the numbers of the 454. Each ship's numbers add up to thirteen. I didn't think much about it until we started talking on the way back to the ship tonight." I could see he didn't want me to think he was superstitious. "I don't think it's serious talk, just scuttlebutt."

I nodded. "Well, we don't want talk like this to get out of hand. Let me know if you hear any more of it." Engler and Hicks agreed.

I told Stauffer about the conversation when he returned from his trip to Philadelphia visiting his wife and son. "They didn't think the talk was serious," I said, "but I guess they thought it significant enough to bring to me. Do you think we should try and do something about it?"

Stauffer had a troubled look on his face and paused before answering. "Did they say who's doing the talking?"

"No, just some of the bridge crew."

"Okay. I'll speak to the captain about it tomorrow."

Our fear was that this kind of thinking could become a self-fulfilling prophecy in the same way a losing team falls into the habit of losing. We didn't want that and agreed to make light of such comments. Of the officers, only Captain Blaser took the comments seriously.

Worse, the talk had already spread throughout the ship. The crew was now absolutely convinced YMS-472 was jinxed.

There was little any of the officers could do but make light of the situation and attempt to dispel the dark cloud that seemed to hang over us.

A few weeks later the war in Europe came to an end. Following brief speculation that we might be discharged, we instead received orders to prepare ourselves for passage to the Pacific theater. We were given three weeks for the shipyard to make the necessary changes and repairs, but our ship had been in dry dock so often there was little to do.

On 1 June under the auspices of the USO we held a combined party at the Hotel Warwick for the crews of our ship and that of YMS-454, which would be with us on the first leg of our trip. The party was well attended and both crews had a wonderful time. Wives and girlfriends came from out of state to spend a pleasant evening with their husbands, fiancés, or boyfriends. My wife and I were approached by a number of the young men to introduce us to their fiancées. Stauffer's wife, Betty, came in from Philadelphia for the party. Blaser attended alone and stood a bit apart from the festivities, as he was wont to do, then he left early. Hobart and Frye both had duty aboard the ship and could not attend. Talley, who was there without his girlfriend, spent the night hanging out with others who were also stag. Harrison's wife was not able to attend. He joined me for some beer, then spent the evening with the other "bachelors."

The USO insisted no hard liquor be permitted so one officer from each of the ships was appointed to confiscate any bottles found. I had that duty for my ship. Rather than pour the liquor down the drain, we elected to personally see to its disposal. Later that night my wife had to assist me back to my ship. It was, in retrospect, a not uncommon send off for a sailor.

Early on the morning of the fifth we were under way. We steamed down the Atlantic coast without incident, arriving at Miami, Florida, eight days later. Blaser arranged for the crew to draw our pay because this would be the first of many ports where the men would receive short liberty. It took three days to reprovision and for the crew to go through a large part of their pay. On 16 June we departed for Guantanamo Bay in Cuba. From there we went to Colon in the Panama Canal zone.

Passing through the canal I'd hoped to visit old friends in Balboa where I'd been stationed in 1944, but we were ordered to head directly to Corinto, Nicaragua. Arriving there on 1 July, we stayed only a day, which was just as well because the crew was broke. One man returned to the ship with a parakeet while two brought back a mangy monkey that they named Tojo. Just as we set sail Frye arrived bearing a coati mundi he'd named Albert. The creature resembled a bear but was no bigger than a cat. YMS-472 was starting to resemble a floating menagerie.

Albert was soon the favorite. He was well mannered and kept to himself. Each day he would find our discarded soft drink bottles and with his long snout lick them clean. He spent his evenings on the bridge and slept in the lap of the officer on watch.

Our next port was Manzanilla, Mexico, a quiet town with a remarkably clear bay. The crew pitched coins, which was about all they had left, and marveled at the youngsters who dove after them. We were under way the next morning and four days later reached San Pedro, California. Alterations were required to some of our equipment to meet the specifications of the Pacific Fleet, so our ship was directed to a civilian shipyard for the changes. This proved to be a holiday resort. We tied up on the main pier of the South Coast Company, the same pier of the personal boat of Humphrey Bogart and Lauren Bacall.

The crew took leave in nearby Newport Beach where Albert established himself as the preeminent draw for attractive young women.

Living nearby, Harrison's wife came to visit. She was joined by Ash's young wife, who had traveled west from Connecticut. None of us knew when we would see family again. These were just wonderful men and I wanted to do something special for them. I arranged to have their wives join them for a private dinner in the officers' wardroom when the other officers were ashore. The cook joined in the spirit of the occasion because these were the only wives we ever had aboard ship. He prepared a special meal. Once again the captain knew of our nonregulation conduct, but he elected to turn a blind eye to it.

We were assigned a new crewman named George Casleton. He was twenty years old, more than six feet tall with a medium build, and was exceptionally handsome. With dark wavy hair, intense eyes, and a deep tan, he was always popular with the ladies and did not require Albert's help. His father was ailing and, I understood, had plans for him to take over the family business after the war, but I could see his love of the lifestyle in California and doubted very much he'd ever go back to the cold Midwest winters. I imagined telling his father that he had other life plans was not going to be easy for him. For now, Casleton enjoyed his popularity with the girls and frolicked in the sand and surf whenever he could. There was little enough time for play for any of us.

At San Pedro one evening, Stauffer had the watch and couldn't leave the ship. When I returned from liberty he asked me to go to the local jail to get Engler, who liked to have a good time and enjoyed his beer, especially so on this occasion. He had been picked up by the shore patrol. This wasn't typical behavior for anyone on our ship and Engler had a sheepish expression when he saw me. "I'm sorry, Mr. Renner," he told me over and over. "Nothing like this will happen again." I told him it was all right. These things happened.

Before leaving San Pedro, Ash found a stray cat, a beautiful all-white female, and brought her aboard. She was playful and came the closest to being a lap cat as I'd ever seen. We never did name her; we just called her "Cat." Albert took a liking to her and they soon were seen running around the ship playing together.

By mid-July we had participated in both antisubmarine and gunnery exercises to allow us to gain some skill with the modified equipment. We performed exceptionally well. Even the captain expressed his satisfaction with the crew. Spirits were high as we drew specific orders to report to the Pacific Fleet. During the following days we practiced emergency shipboard procedures, including damage control, abandoning ship, man overboard, and fire fighting. We were finally ordered to set sail for Pearl Harbor, Hawaii, on 5 August.

Joining us for the passage were three other minesweepers: YMS-454, YMS-292, and YMS-436. We four made up the entire convoy. Our chart course from San Pedro was 256. The crew did not miss the sums of each of these numbers. Thirteen was the common total. In addition, our estimated arrival date at Pearl was 13 August. Someone noted it had taken us thirteen days to travel from New York to Panama, then thirteen days from Panama to San Pedro. The ship and crew were performing splendidly. My fellow officers and I had sincerely hoped that all such talk was behind us.

The coincidence of all this, however, became the routine gossip of the ship. Some of the crew were so spooked by what was happening that Blaser called a meeting of the officers.

Using a concocted excuse, we decided to ask the port director to pull us from this convoy and allowed us to depart with the next. Our request was denied.

Now a sense of uneasiness permeated the ship. Blaser's request, though well intended, had given his official sanction to the superstitions of some of the crew. There was persistent talk of a jinx accompanying us. We officers treated it all in a casual manner but it did not have the desired effect.

We journeyed toward the Hawaiian Islands in a loose convoy, keeping within sight of one another but not establishing any fixed position. The crew had taken so much liberty in the previous weeks that the daily contact on the small ship proved taxing. The natural antipathy between the deck crew and engine room crew reasserted itself. The ship carried only a three-day supply of fresh water. We relied on our evaporators to produce more, although they were not able to provide for all our needs. As a consequence water had to be rationed and the evaporators ran around the clock, placing a burden on the engine room crew. There was disagreement over water usage by the deck crew, and this led to a heightening of tension among the men.

On the morning of the fifth day the sea was rough and the sky overcast. On the horizon was the landing ship tank (LST) with which our minesweeper was scheduled to rendezvous for refueling. This was accomplished with some difficulty and our journey continued on in a somber mood.

Although we were far out to sea we were not cut off from the world. On 9 August I was standing watch very early in the morning under quite pleasant circumstances. There was an agreeable breeze. Albert was nestled inside my jacket sleeping. I was up on the flying bridge with the lighthearted Engler, always a good man with whom to stand watch. We were listening to music Hobart had tuned in for us. At about 0300 a news flash interrupted the broadcast. It was President Harry Truman announcing the dropping of the first atomic bomb on Japan. We were very excited initially but the more we talked about it the more persuaded we became that the bombing of Hiroshima and Nagasaki a few days later could very well incite the Japanese to become even more aggressive. We knew about the suicide bombings of our ships and expected even more fanaticism. Our final opinion was that sweeping the approaches for the invasion of Japan was going to be very dangerous work.

We arrived in Pearl Harbor on 13 August, as scheduled. While there I was awakened one morning and informed that the war with Japan was over. Learning the war had ended, and so unexpectedly, was one of the most exciting moments of my life. I was jubilant, as was everyone else onboard ship and throughout the city. We all joined in a wild celebration. Any thought of the number thirteen was forgotten. We were going home.

Calmer heads pointed out that a lot of minesweeping still had to be done. The end of the war did not automatically make mines already in place suddenly disappear. We convinced ourselves the regular navy would be assigned the job and figured we'd be sent straight home from Pearl. Instead, our departure to the Pacific Fleet was only delayed for two days. Unfortunately for Albert, Cat jumped ship before we left.

We practiced routine procedures en route to occupy the crew, but the persistent talk was of our plans for the future. It made no sense to us to remain in the navy a day longer than necessary. There had been rumors about a point system, which would determine everyone's release date, and it only added to the speculation about our future. We arrived at Eniwetok six days later, then left for Saipan the next morning.

When I was stationed in Panama I had served on the Pacific side of the isthmus. During the time I was there the seas were calm and warm, and the occasional storm was really not much more than an afternoon rain shower. The water was light blue, quite pleasant, and moved in shallow swells. It was as kind an introduction to the sea as one could imagine.

New York harbor in the North Atlantic was much colder and darker in color. I was there during the winter and spring when the water was choppy almost constantly. When there was a storm we easily found shelter in the harbor.

Sailing now to Okinawa I had all but crossed the vast Pacific during the summer. Again I had found the water warm and a pleasant blue. It moved with generally predictable swells that hinted of the ocean's immense power but bore our small ship gently along. All in all, I thought during the long hours of watch, I'd been lucky.

The Pacific crossing had many touching moments. We were such a small ship, in so vast an ocean, you couldn't help but be humbled by the experience. Often when I stood watch I'd see a crewman standing alone, as alone as it is possible to be in such cramped circumstances, staring across the water. For some it was just a quiet moment to smoke a cigarette while waiting for the next work assignment—but not for everyone.

I would see George Wade like this. He was from West Virginia and came from a large, close-knit family. I don't think he'd ever been away from home before and was often homesick. He received more mail than anyone else aboard YMS-472. He tended to stay apart from the rest of the crew, not because he was a loner, far from it, but I think because he was so removed from his natural element and maybe perhaps a bit in awe of his surroundings. In New York he had often stayed aboard even though he was due liberty. Whenever I saw him alone on the stern, gazing back across the ocean, I knew he was thinking of home. It was such times that added so much to our sense of family.

At Saipan the captain informed us that two of our crew were eligible for immediate discharge, although they wouldn't leave until our next stop. Chief Gunners Mate Fits, who'd first reported the handgun missing when the ship was commissioned, was one who would soon leave. At Saipan for a few days, the crew enjoyed liberty. Stauffer and I examined a few caves where the bitter fighting had taken place and I was glad I'd joined the navy. Liberty was especially satisfying for the crew that day as the crews of the four ships in our group had a picnic and played softball games. Beer was also served on that warm summer day of 1 September. It was one of the happiest in the short career of YMS-472.

We were directed to proceed to Okinawa on 6 September. From there we would participate in sweeping the Inland Sea of Japan free of mines. We traveled with the same three minesweepers. Endless discussions took place about the new point system and how soon any more of us would be leaving for home. We dropped anchor in Buckner Bay, Okinawa, on 13 September, joining hundreds of other ships at anchor there. The island was approximately 450 miles south and west of the southernmost tip of Japan. It was a narrow island some seventy miles long, five to ten miles in width.

Okinawa had been the site of the bloodiest Pacific battle of the war, lasting from 1 April until 2 July, ending not that many weeks prior to our arrival. More than sixteen thousand Americans and an estimated one hundred thousand Japanese had died there. From the harbor we could see little of the island except for the haphazard clustering of temporary structures that had been hastily erected by the U.S. Army. There was no liberty so we set about routine ship duty and repairs.

Two more of the crew now had sufficient points to qualify for immediate discharge: Shockley and Frye. Unfortunately, there was no one available to take their places so they were to remain with us for the days or weeks it would take for the navy to find suitable replacements.

It had been a long passage across the Pacific for such a small vessel not designed for service away from the coast. We had traveled somewhere between six and seven thousand miles. Many repairs were required before we would be fit for duty. Our evaporator, which had been in nearly continuous use since leaving New York, needed the most service. We really weren't equipped to work on it, but our request to have it repaired was denied and we were told to perform the overhaul ourselves. I'd worked on the devices with Frye, who with his recent promotion was now in charge of the two engine rooms, and other crewmen from time to time while under way with no results. Blaser instructed that we set about all repairs as quickly as we could.

Regardless of our duties or whether or not we were standing watch, the talk remained focused on our futures once we were back home. I'd already written my previous employer to inquire about my job. My daughter was now fourteen months old and I hardly knew her. For that matter, I hadn't spent all that much time with my new wife either.

The weather was magnificent and 15 September was an especially beautiful day with scattered cumulus clouds. The harbor was still and there was scarcely a breeze off the ocean. The temperature hovered at 80 degrees. The ship's crew was jovial and busy with the customary chipping and painting. Others washed laundry and hung it about. I spent the day working primarily with Frye, Harrison, and Ash on the problematic evaporator.

I stood an early watch and smoked a quiet cigar on the fantail, discussing civilian plans with the usual suspects. Albert was nosing about, hunting down empty soda bottles. We had received word that our command ship, an auxiliary minesweeper (AM), would be showing *Rhapsody in Blue* that night and all off-duty personnel were invited to watch it. Liberty ashore was not available so it was either see the movie or stay on our own small vessel. The setting sun briefly reflected like a mirror off the calm water.

That night was, if anything, more beautiful than the day. I'd seen the movie before but enjoyed it once again. Forty or fifty men were in attendance, sitting on folding chairs arranged in neat rows. The movie ended at 2100 and we headed back to our ship on a small gig. Skimming across the glassy water I observed how still the bay was. It was difficult to imagine the harbor was part of a vast ocean. Tonight it was so much like a millpond. We had heard there was a storm well southeast of us near Guam, but there was no sign of it here. There was no wind, none at all. We joked lightly about the contrast.

The crew was in an amiable mood. There were card games in progress and I kibitzed a bit before going to the small officers' quarters. Boyd Stauffer, who had become my closest friend, was up for a hand of rummy. We normally kept a running tab on our betting. At the moment I owed him five dollars and I was determined to reverse my state of affairs. We talked about his wife and their new son. He was more than ready for his discharge and eager to get home to his life with his family.

We briefly discussed the distant storm but gave it no special attention. The previous year there had been two very violent typhoons in the Pacific that had caused heavy damage to

American fleets, but we had not heard about them because we were stationed in the Atlantic at the time. Hobart, stretched out as much as our small wardroom allowed, was reading. He allowed that it "'tis the season" for such storms. Just as hurricanes have their time of year in the Atlantic so too did the Pacific version, here called a typhoon. I made no progress on my card debt with the smiling Stauffer. I decided to go to bed and I was soon fast asleep.

THREE

Typhoon

At 0530 on 16 September 1945 I was startled from my sleep. "You gotta get up right now, Mr. Renner!" a voice shouted. "A typhoon is coming our way, and we've been ordered to put out to sea as soon as possible!"

It was Cox'n Mate Jerry Doring. He was one of the least excitable men onboard and the manner in which he spoke told me more than his words. Apparently the storm we had discussed so casually the previous night had unexpectedly turned and was now headed toward us. Stauffer hurried out of his bunk. As he quickly dressed we commented on Doring's state. If someone as solid as Jerry was rattled we knew something serious was going on.

Once Stauffer was out the door there was room for me to dress. Before I finished Blaser stepped in. His manner was very calm, as if we were about to begin a routine day. "Elm, we have to get under way because of an approaching typhoon."

I told him Doring had just notified me. "We have parts of the evaporator scattered all over the forward engine deck," I said. "It may take a little while to secure them but we'll get the engines warmed up while we're picking things up. Do you know anything about the storm?"

Blaser shook his head. "Only that it's approaching from the south. Let's get going. The message said urgent."

I had almost finished dressing. "Do you know where we're going, or are we just going to ride it out?" I didn't like the sound of those words.

"We haven't got word yet but will probably hear something before we clear harbor." With that he left.

Blaser hadn't seemed especially disturbed by our sudden switch in plans, but even in my cramped quarters I could feel the changes aboard ship. The sense of urgency was absolutely electric. Outside the room I saw Doring again and was struck by how a usually very competent man was suddenly uncertain and tentative.

I passed through the wardroom where the steward's mate was busy stowing items away. I grabbed a cup of black coffee but soon set it down. I never got a chance to drink it. I checked outside and was startled that such a profound change could have taken place in so short a time. Two hundred feet above us, blackish gray clouds, boiling and rolling, were being driven by very strong winds across a sky the color of slate. The sea below was black, white caps crowning the crest of small waves. The numerous ships in the harbor were rocking back and forth on their lines in the choppy water and gusting wind. I could sense the power in the coming storm, and a sensation of urgency and anticipation such as I'd never experienced before shot through my body.

Buckner Bay, where we were anchored, was on the south-east side of Okinawa and the storm appeared to be coming directly at us. If we stayed where we were we'd be slammed onto the shore and the ship would be broken apart. The standard procedure in such a situation was for a vessel to ride the storm out far to sea, away from threatening land. This assumed, of course, that the ship was able to withstand the power of the storm. The alternative was to shelter in a safe harbor with the mass of the island *toward* the storm, to brunt the wind and offer protection from the waves.

The deck crew was hurriedly preparing for departure. Clothes were down, the scattered paint cans had disappeared, cases of Coke were no longer in sight. Anything that might come loose was being stowed away or secured. Everything that could be done was and in as competent a manner as possible. The laxity that had crept over us since the end of the war had vanished in the face of the approaching storm.

My duties were to see that all tools and other free objects were secured in the engine rooms. Things were going at a fever pitch as the engine crew went about its duty without orders from me. Shortly the five-hundred-horsepower diesel engines would be fired up so we'd be ready to put to sea when the order was given.

Based on my experience with the hurricane in Jacksonville, I thought I had some idea of what we were facing. I did not consider that the Florida hurricane had been a hurricane on land where its force was attenuated. Typhoons in the vast expanse of the Pacific are much more powerful than Atlantic hurricanes. What was about to occur bore no meaningful resemblance to my previous experience.

Feeling the rocking of the ship, and considering what I had seen outside, my feelings were mixed. I felt a certain anticipation at the thought of riding out a typhoon in the open sea in such a small ship. We would be facing danger, something that had been very lacking in my service so far. It was going to be exciting, the ride of a lifetime. The thought that we could not survive did not occur to me—not yet.

I checked the forward engine room, which housed the large generator for magnetic minesweeping, two auxiliary power generators, the fresh water evaporator, and the main electrical panel. Some of the engine room men were busy stowing the tools and parts we had left scattered there from our work on the evaporator and I pitched in. As we finished I felt the low rumble of the two main engines and informed the bridge we were ready to put out to sea.

Although we had worked expeditiously to prepare for sea there had been no exceptional rush because we had been given no additional information about the rapidly approaching storm. We were making preparations as quickly as possible but had been taking our time to do everything by the book. Our pace was the same as that of the other ships anchored in the bay so there was no sense of our being left behind. Had we been ordered to clear the harbor at once, the stowing could have waited and we'd have been under way much faster than we were. But we received no such order.

Finally, we were nearly ready. When we tried to retrieve the first anchor a heavy groan came from the winch motor as it slowed to a stall. Killing the power, we maneuvered the ship closer to the bulky anchor. It made no difference. We moved the ship again, placing it directly above the anchor but the motor was still unable to raise it. The anchor simply wouldn't budge; it was snagged on something on the harbor bottom. We took nearly a half hour working at the anchor before finally decid-ing to abandon the effort and released the chain.

The second anchor was also fouled, but with just the one line we were able to maneuver the ship with greater freedom. We soon had it freed. Given the increased power of the storm there seemed to be no more time to spare. While we had wres-tled with the anchors the winds had increased considerably and the waves had grown in height and intensity. Blaser advised the command ship that we were ready and was given orders to clear the harbor. We quickly joined one of the two long lines of ships that were clearing the harbor, making for the open sea. Blaser ordered everyone to put on a life jacket.

Our instructions were to sail northeast along the east coast of Okinawa. This route took us on the side of the island facing the storm but it was the most direct course to our destination. We were to go around the north tip of the island, then sail southwest until we came to a smaller but more protected bay named Unten Ko. This would place us leeward of the island where we would be sheltered from the high winds by the raised ground surrounding the bay. There we could wait out the storm in safety. I estimated the bay was about a hundred miles away. Looking at the storm outside I doubted that we were going to make it. We needed ten to twelve hours' sailing time and we just didn't have it, not with the speed at which the gale was closing in on us.

The ship just ahead of us was a net tender, tailing a sub-marine chaser. To starboard was a minesweeper even smaller than our ship. We all followed the marked channel, sailing toward the open sea. The winds increased considerably as we moved from the bay and the waves were far more menacing.

Still, this was a unique event for all of us and we were excited about what we were seeing and experiencing. Spirits were high and there were more sick grins than expressions of fear. Stauffer urged me to get out my movie camera but I told him I was going to wait. Things would get a lot wilder once we were farther out. Our mess cook brought crackers, sardines, and apples to the bridge, standard fare for a rough sea lunch. I passed on food because I tended to be seasick the first day at sea and didn't want to run the risk. It wasn't raining yet but the winds were picking up and the seas were getting heavier with each passing minute. This was going to be some ride.

As we rounded the last channel marker and entered the open sea we altered course as ordered to run approximately parallel to the southeast coast of Okinawa. The other ships in line turned with us and with more room began to spread out. No one wanted to inadvertently ram one of the other ships. A moderate rain had now joined the gusting wind. In this new arrangement only a few ships remained in view.

I was on the flying bridge, which had the best visibility, and could see that the submarine chaser was having a very rough time. The storm was now so violent that there were moments when most of the ship was under water. The vessel rocked with the waves and its screws popped into the open, something that was never supposed to happen. Our own engines were racing every time we went over the crest of a wave and I realized that our screws were coming out of the water as well. I wondered for a moment how we looked to the other ships and experienced my first sense of genuine unease.

Waves were now crashing over our starboard beam, causing the small ship to roll side to side. The rolls extended 30 to 35 degrees, quite heavy, and though I'd experienced them before, never with such frequency. This caused an immediate change in the mood of the crew and the lopsided grins vanished. There were no more wisecracks, less talk, and a look of concern appeared on every face. This was no party and everyone, including me, now understood it.

The wind was whipping quite strongly by now. Outside the drops of water struck exposed skin with the sting of an insect bite. The sky was growing darker and the seas much rougher. The rain rapidly increased until it interfered with our visibility. We had been through storms before, powerful storms off the North Atlantic, but we had always had access to New York harbor for a haven. Here in the vast Pacific, now that we had been forced out of Buckner Bay, there was nothing to spare us from the force of the typhoon.

The storm, named by the Japanese the Makurazaki typhoon, had begun on 10 September fourteen hundred miles south and east of Okinawa. It would be nearly fifty years before there was another of such great power. The typhoon changed directions more than once but ran the characteristic path of such storms, making its way north and west. Five hundred miles in diameter, it moved across the face of the ocean at various speeds, ranging from ten to fifteen miles per hour. Sustained winds were 135 miles per hour with reports of gusts even higher. As late as 0300 on 16 September forecasts had the typhoon passing 275 miles southwest of Okinawa. At that distance it would have been no threat to us. But the storm had turned unexpectedly toward us and suddenly increased speed to sixteen to eighteen miles per hour.

I knew none of this at the time. I stuck my head into the engine room, then went to the small main bridge. Most, although not all, of the crew had positioned themselves there, or within the much smaller radar shack or chart room immediately behind it. Few wanted to be outside in the storm. I was starting to feel queasy and feared a bout of seasickness. I couldn't see going outside and leaning over the rail under such conditions and I certainly didn't want to throw up inside.

Fear of the storm had not as yet taken over and there was considerable chatter on the main bridge with Harrison, not surprisingly, doing most of the talking. Clearly excited, he spoke at a higher pitch than usual. Several crew members sitting on the deck looked a lot more sober. "Hey," Harrison said pointing out a port, "look over there! See that one! What a sight! I hope nothing like that strikes us broadside."

Shockley was on the wheel, spinning it first one direction then the other, working to keep us on course. His eyes darted from one side to the other, searching out large waves, then dropped to the clicking gyro to check his heading. "If it ever does," he said without looking at Harrison, "that would be it for us." He suddenly spun the wheel to nose the ship into a wave.

Harrison was undisturbed. "We sure didn't have these when we were in New York. Hey, Renner, did you ever see anything like this when you were in Panama?"

"No, and I hope not to see too many of them out here either."

"Who's on duty in the engine room?" he asked.

"Hasberg," I told him. "I hope he doesn't get seasick again." Like me, Pete Hasberg was also prone to seasickness. "I was down there a few minutes ago and Hasberg looked pretty peaked, but I think he'll be all right."

"If he does, I'll replace him," Harrison volunteered.

"No need, Bill. He'll make it." A good man had the next watch so I wasn't concerned.

One of the men shouted in an excited voice. "Look at that ship over there! I wonder if we look like that. Look, you can see its rudder and screws coming right out of the water!"

Harrison said, "I'm sure ours do too. A little while ago I could feel it as we went over a big wave."

I had felt it many times already but saw no reason to add to the general concern. The captain, Stauffer, and our signalman Engler were above us on the flying bridge. Although there was a four-foot bulkhead around it they were largely exposed to the storm. None of the other ships could now be seen. The sky had become a dark and austere gray. The clouds and water were jet black. The wind, rain, and heavy seas were increasing in intensity and we were now being struck directly broadside on our starboard beam. I could no longer tell if the sheets of water washing over us were driving rain or sea water lifted from the crests of the waves. It was probably a mix of both.

We were perhaps four or five miles off shore and the difference between being anchored in a protected bay and being on the open sea was very apparent. Waves were now thirty to forty feet high and blocked our visibility beyond a few hundred yards. The ocean rose and fell in great swaths, which moved in opposing directions like immense pistons. The bow of the ship plunged into the heavy seas and water crashed over the main deck, submerging it beneath swirls of white foam and black water for ever longer periods of time. Crewmen were pressed against the glass of the portholes, staring transfixed into the storm, their increasingly dull eyes absorbing the power of the growing waves and sight of the ominous sky. It was only midafternoon but already dark enough to be night.

The wind and waves grew in size and severity to the point where exposure to the storm on the deck became increasingly dangerous. We received orders from Blaser that no one was to be below the main deck or in the open. This meant the main bridge, radio shack, and chart room—the only enclosed areas above deck—were all going to be very crowded as those already there were joined by the handful who had been below. There was a single door leading from each room to the main bridge.

It was a wise order but brought to me a moment of apprehension. The two greatest fears for sailors from time immemorial are fire or to be capsized. Fire at sea is nearly always deadly and often destroys the ship and crew. Capsizing is inevitably deadly. Any seamen below are suddenly trapped, with no way out. Those on the deck are swept into violent seas. Any vessel that capsized usually sank within moments, with heavy loss of life.

The ship's constant rolling caused by the waves striking us broadside was our most serious concern because this motion represented our greatest danger. The ship's inclinometer was now registering rolls of 40 degrees. I knew we were designed to withstand rolls substantially in excess of that, but I had no desire to test its boundary. Even rolls of 40 degrees, repeated often enough, were perilous for us. Blaser ordered that we alter course so the waves were not striking us so directly on starboard but more off the bow. We also reduced speed slightly to lessen our impact with the waves. This slowed us but there really wasn't anything else to do.

On occasion we could see the top of the mast of one of the other ships fighting the storm. From time to time we spotted an entire vessel carried disturbingly high on the crest of an enormous wave. We attempted to make radio contact with other ships but were unable to do so. I had never experienced anything like this.

Altering course and speed had improved our situation a bit and the rolling moderated slightly. Now we were sustaining a combination of a roll and a pitch, commonly called a yaw; that is, the ship was dipping down into the water, then rocking back up on her stern as well as rolling side to side. When we plowed into a wave, our bow appearing to dive into a whirling wall, immense sheets of water broke across the bow, slapping the superstructure with such force the bridge shuddered in a way I'd never felt before. It was profoundly disconcerting.

A familiar queasy feeling engulfed me and I was suddenly seasick. I hurried out into the storm and made my way precariously to the railing. When I was finished I clawed my way below to my bunk, sensing the uneasiness of the ship, staggering against motions I'd never before experienced, clinging to whatever solid object presented itself to stay on my feet. I climbed into my bunk with the hope that by laying down my condition would improve. I had no duties to perform at the moment but was due to stand a four-hour watch starting at midnight. I needed to be recovered by then.

My initial exhilaration had turned to fear and there was no possibility of sleep. It seemed to me that it was very likely that we would sink if this kept up. What was to happen to my family then? I took photographs of my wife and daughter from my wallet. Clutching the side of the bunk as the shipped rocked I gazed at their faces. Would I ever see them again in the flesh? My civilian job was promised to me. All I had ever wanted since before I had been called up was a normal life, with a normal family. I'd had enough travel, and even by now, enough excitement to last a lifetime. I had a very uneasy feeling about the fate of our ship.

Below the foredeck, out of sight of the storm, was worse than it had been on the bridge. Every few moments a sudden, violent movement of the ship interrupted my thoughts. I gripped the sides of my bunk and held on until each violent episode passed. The extravagant motions never came to an end and the increasingly severe rolls were causing me serious concern. The gale was seriously testing the seaworthiness of the ship. How many times could a ship of this size roll so far? What if one of the hatches popped open or a plank in the hull burst and we started taking on water? There would come a time with the hold heavy with sea water when she'd lose her ability to right herself and we'd just keep rolling right over.

I had never doubted the quality of the ship previously, but this was, after all, an all-wood vessel. How much of a beating could her hull sustain? In such violent conditions could the oak ribs take the pounding without yielding to the forces? I didn't know but I had my doubts. They had started making ships out of metal for a reason.

We'd been through storms before, tough ones I'd thought at the time, but nothing like this. The main difference now was the suddenness of the violence and how pronounced the ship's motion had become. The roll of a ship can be fast or slow but until now the rolls had always been like the swing of the pendulum of a clock. A ship usually moves at a steady rate through a complete and predictable cycle.

These rolls were violent in the extreme. It was as if a normal roll had been interrupted by an incredible shock, as if the ship had suddenly been forced to change direction by the overwhelming power of the sea. It didn't seem possible that anything so small constructed by man could continue to withstand such forces.

All the talk that this was an unlucky ship came back to me as I lay there. I had never given it serious thought but now wondered if there wasn't something to it. What could the odds be of such a long string of thirteens? They had to be enormous. The longer the ship shuddered and rolled, and the more I dwelled on the thirteens, the more I became resigned to the thought that the ship could not survive this pounding. My life and that of my shipmates depended on whether the storm would abate, or leave us in its wake before the ship succumbed. If the typhoon lasted long enough it was only a matter of time. It was very likely that YMS-472 was a doomed ship.

I closed my eyes, although the worsening conditions meant I couldn't sleep. The rolling and pitching, the sound of the waves striking the ship's hull, the cascading of water on the bulkhead of my quarters, all reminded me of the reality.

The raging storm was testing the seaworthiness of the ship in ways none of us had ever imagined. I tried to think again about my wife Dorothy and daughter Pat, but instead I dwelled increasingly on visions of disaster. What was going to happen? Was it even possible to make a safe harbor at this point? If not, could we ride out a storm of such incredible violence?

I wondered if there was anything more that the damage control team could do. Were there orders I should give? Any preparations I should see to? I couldn't think of anything. I realized I was trying to fight off the reality of my predicament. I was helpless, at the utter mercy of the typhoon, and just didn't want to face it.

Without warning the ship's violent reaction to a massive wave striking us broadside threw me out of my bunk, landing me sprawling on the deck of my quarters. The ship lay on its side so far and for so long I was certain we had capsized. I remained on the deck gripped by absolute terror. The ship hung there, as if suspended in time, unmoving, then slowly, very, very slowly, she began to right herself.

Using the door of my locker I pulled myself into the lower bunk and tried to comprehend what had just happened. My seasickness had vanished. Facing your own mortality even for a moment will do that. Suddenly I was panicked. I didn't want to be trapped in my quarters if the ship capsized. The idea of finding myself upside down within the ship, the black sea water rushing in, no escape, filled me with renewed terror. I had to get out of here. I pulled my rain gear out of the locker and clawed my way into it. Grabbing my life jacket I headed for the bridge. If I was meant to die it wasn't going to be down here, trapped like a rat in a box.

The cramped officers' wardroom was a mess even though we'd prepared it for sea. Books, playing cards, and other debris were scattered everywhere. I hesitated for an instant, instinctively starting to clean up, then realized that was futile. I passed through the mess then ascended the ladder that led directly to the main bridge.

There was an eerie quiet as I stepped on deck within the bridge. There were now perhaps a dozen men in the small room. Several were peering out the portholes as if hypnotized while others were sitting on the deck, holding onto anything available, their bodies rocking with the unpredictable motion of the ship. No one spoke. Outside was the crashing of the waves but inside the only sound came from the gyrocompass repeater clicking off the constant minor change of direction of the ship as Shockley frantically spun the wheel to bring the ship back on course.

I checked the inclinometer, which held a record of the steepest roll we'd taken up until now, and couldn't believe what I was seeing. *Seventy-three* degrees! *My God!* I thought. Everyone there saw what I was doing. They knew what the instrument said. No one commented. But YMS-472 had taken it.

I took a quick look at the faces of the young men in the bridge and could see the fear in their eyes, in the set of their mouth, the gray pallor of their skin. They'd been as scared as I had. Our lives were at stake and everyone knew it. More than one had a look of pure panic. For an instant I thought about what it had been like here, where they could see the water.

The faces turned toward me, begging for some words of hope, anything that would dispel the gnawing fear and gloom that filled the air. There really were no words, at least not words that would make everything right, which is what they really wanted. I smiled weakly, "Something to tell our grandchildren."

No one reacted. Not one. I realized that they could see in my eyes what I saw in theirs.

FOUR

Mountains

Quartermaster Shockley continued to man the helm. He furiously spun the wheel, first to port, then to starboard. His eyes darted between watching the gyro repeater and being on the lookout for oncoming waves, doing his best to maintain course and still prevent the ship from exposure to dangerous broadside waves. From what I could see the waves had more control over the direction of the ship than the rudders.

"What's our heading?" I asked.

"Zero-seven-zero," Shockley answered, never taking his eyes from the gyro.

Our course had been zero-six-zero so I asked why the change. He replied that the captain had ordered the course change a few minutes earlier in another attempt to minimize the rolling.

"What the hell happened?" I asked.

"I saw this wave coming straight at us and tried to head into it, but, unlike the others, it came on so quickly the ship didn't have time to respond and hit us almost broadside. I was hanging on to the wheel and my feet went right out from under me. The captain ordered the course change right after that."

Talley, who was very agitated, said, "Damn, that was close! I was sure we were goners! We all ended up against the port bulkhead!" His eyes were wide in excitement and fear.

Harrison jumped in. "We've got to do something." Of course, that was our real problem. We *did* have to do something before the sea got us—but there was absolutely nothing we could do.

"Has anyone heard from Frye?" I asked.

"No," Harrison said.

"Give him a call to see if he's okay."

Talley grabbed the intercom. I could hear Frye's voice from where I stood. "Jesus Christ," he shouted, "what's going on up there?" Talley told him what had happened.

Blaser called down from the flying bridge. "Everyone okay down there?"

"Yeah, we're all right," Shockley answered. "How about you guys? Did you see it coming?"

"Yes," the captain said, "but too late to do anything about it. We damn near lost Engler overboard. He's okay though."

I looked out the portholes and took a good look at what Shockley was trying to cope with. This was the first time I had actually set eyes on the storm since going below. The winds then had been sixty miles an hour, with heavy rain and waves of thirty to forty feet. The wind had multiplied and both the rain and the seas were now substantially more powerful.

What especially struck me was how vicious the water looked and how violently the ship was reacting to it. The water boiled like a vast cauldron, white foam dancing on the surface in crazy patterns. We were rolling to one side or another continuously but waves would strike us from the direction we were moving like a massive fist, causing the ship to abruptly stop with a great shudder, then change direction. The ship was withstanding a terrific beating.

As I watched, it looked as if the bow was diving into waves, taking a tremendous volume of water across us, creating a huge spray that shot forty or fifty feet into the air, completely shrouding the ship. Talley was manning the annunciator, which called for two-thirds ahead. At that setting, under normal conditions, we would have been making seven to eight knots. It was impossible to know how fast we were actually moving in these conditions because the wind and waves had as much to do with it as our screws.

Although only midafternoon, the impression was that we were already into night. The eye of the storm was moving due north and headed directly at us, but we had no way of knowing that. The Makurazaki typhoon was traveling at eighteen miles an hour. It was just 110 miles south of our position. As the storm approached and we were subjected to increasingly furious winds, our condition worsened. The ship continued her constant extreme rolls and even more disturbing to me was the now almost routine shudder I felt pass through the supple wood hull as she reacted to the forces thrown against her.

With personnel transfers we were a bit shorthanded. Our crew of thirty-six had been reduced to thirty-one. A total of twenty-seven were on the small bridge, radio shack, and chart room. I made my way to the radio shack to see if we had established any communication. Hobart was talking with another ship, but he had no idea where she was. He said he thought she was pretty close although we could no longer see any of the other ships fighting the storm. They didn't know anything more than we did.

By now we had been sailing on a northeasterly course up the coast of Okinawa for five to six hours. Without the storm we would have been two-thirds of the way to the northern tip of the island, where we were scheduled to make our turn toward the safe harbor of Unten Ko. With this in mind I entered the radar room to see if I could determine our location. Our radar was primitive. The operator was switching back and forth between the two settings but could see nothing that shed any light as to our location. The radar was cluttered with reflections off the rain, mist, and blowing water, making it impossible to make out any distinguishing characteristics of the coast. Hobart told me he hadn't had a fix on the island in hours.

Despite the conditions the captain, Engler, and Stauffer were still atop on the mostly exposed flying bridge, the place with the best visibility. I decided to join them. I could exit the bridge on either the port or starboard side. The port side seemed safer because the heaviest waves were coming at us from the starboard side, so I went out that way. I grabbed hold of the rail as I exited the bridge and descended the four steps to the fore deck. From there it was only a few hurried steps to the bottom of the ladder, which led to the roof of the radio shack. I was always on the lee side of the wind yet it whipped around the superstructure with tremendous power. I grabbed the rails of the ladder and carefully climbed it to near the top. On the last rung of the ladder, a powerful gust of wind and a sheet of solid spray struck me with the force of a blow, nearly sweeping me away. I clung to the two stanchions, mounted on the roof just above the ladder rails, with all my might and pulled myself against the ladder, hugging it with every bit of strength I had. Slowly, I regained my balance, then braced myself and staggered across the roof. I made it to the flying bridge and joined Blaser, Engler, and Stauffer.

They were huddled at the forward bulkhead, ducking the heavy spray, which was now a nearly solid wall of water. The cowling surrounding the top of the superstructure was designed to deflect wind and spray from entering the flying bridge. It was as if it didn't exist. When they rose to view the storm they held on to the rail in front or clung to another gyro repeater mounted nearby on a pedestal. Every few seconds the ship's bow plunged into the next wave and water washed over us in a great surge. From here I could see the full fury of the storm, how wild the waves had grown, how angry the waters. The winds were now routinely lifting water from the surface, mixing it with the rain and spray. The scene was as shocking as when I'd been thrown from my bunk earlier.

I'd never experienced winds and seas like this before. Waves rose and fell like ponderous mountains and the sound was horrendous. The howling wind was far beyond anything I had ever heard before and the crashing water beat on the ship with a constant dreadful banging. I could see waves upon waves, smaller ones dancing across huge ones, waves of every description coming at us from all directions. When a massive wave struck to the starboard the ship would go into a violent roll and give off a lingering shudder. She would hold herself on the edge as if deciding if she was going to keep going, before slowly righting, usually to be struck solidly by a wall of water from the other direction, a staggering force that brought her up cold. Every time was gut wrenching and was repeated again within moments. It was unimaginable.

It was impossible to determine how big any of the waves were because there was nothing against which to measure them. Single waves now commonly rose above our ship's mast, which rose fifty feet above the water line. When the ship slipped temporarily into a trough the tops of the waves loomed well above us.

Each man acknowledged me as I joined him. "How's the crew?" Blaser asked, shouting in short bursts to be heard above the raging wind. Normal conversation was impossible.

I met his eye. "Frightened," I shouted. Well, we were all scared. I could see it in their eyes as well but there was no point in talking about it. Only a lunatic would have been without fear.

The last official word on the storm that we had received had been before the ship cleared Buckner Bay and was hopelessly obsolete. "Typhoon coming from the south" was what it had said. There was no question the gale was drawing closer to us. For hours the captain and Stauffer had been calculating our position by dead reckoning. Their best estimate was that we were twenty to twenty-five miles south of the northern tip of Okinawa. That meant another two or three hours of this before we could even consider making the turn. I didn't believe it was possible for our ship to withstand such forces that long.

"Boyd," I shouted. "Do you think it's letting up?"

Stauffer flashed a nervous smile. "I wish it were, but I can't see any evidence that it is. The captain and I have been talking about riding the storm out at sea. That big roll was too close to risk staying on this course."

"I know. It threw me out of my bunk. The guys below look pretty worried to me. Did you know the inclinometer registered 73 degrees? The ship's only designed for something like sixty. I don't know how we recovered."

Blaser leaned over. "We're thinking about changing base course to head directly into the storm and ride it out. It can't last much longer. What do you think?"

"I don't want to take another wave like that last one. I didn't know things were this bad. Do we know anything about where the storm center is or where it's going?"

The captain had a very stern, tight-lipped expression as he said, "Nothing more than what we knew this morning. It's coming from the south. I think we're going to change course and ride it out. I don't think we can risk another wave like that last one, and I don't think this thing is over yet."

In making this decision, Blaser had given up any hope of reaching Unten Ko. Even if we found the passage between the islands under these conditions, it would have been incredibly dangerous for us to attempt it because we lacked the control over the ship that we would need. The new plan was to turn directly into the waves that were coming most powerfully from the southeast. We'd head into the storm, taking the water over our bow, a vastly preferable option compared to taking it across our beam. We could then reverse course and ride with the seas until we approached the island, then again reverse course. This would relieve the ship from the constant excessive and dangerous rolls that were increasing in severity and frequency. We would, in essence, hold a course as the typhoon spent its fury and passed us by.

There was wisdom in this plan. We had been in the harbor long enough to take on a full supply of fuel, enough to last for more days than the storm. The burden on the ship would be lessened and the dangerous rolls minimized as much as the storm allowed. It would have been better to have simply turned tail and run from the storm but Okinawa blocked us and made that choice impossible—plus it assumed we could travel faster than the storm.

In making his decision, Blaser was severely hampered by his lack of knowledge about the typhoon. Had he known its course and speed he could have intelligently responded. Lacking that, he was compelled to guess.

Blaser called down a new course of one-two-five, in effect a 60-degree turn that aimed us to the southeast, directly into the largest and most powerful waves. As the ship slowly responded to the rudder, I could tell the difference almost at once. We had immediate improved control over the ship and the perilous rolling was suddenly not so extreme. There was, however, an increase in the powerful forces YMS-472 was withstanding as she nosed into the waves. She was taking the massive waves with her bow and bearing the force of the water along her length, rather than across her side. Our situation now was not as perilous. But the visual image, of the waves striking our ship and the inundating cascading mass of the solid water as it roared along the ship, nearly submerging her, was terrifying.

The primary problem with the plan and our new course was that it meant we had given up all hope of finding safe harbor and our course was taking us directly into the power of the typhoon. We were now committed to the storm—and whatever fate it held for us.

We lost our gyrocompass while I was on the flying bridge. The repeaters were not responding to our nearly constant changes in direction caused by the wind and waves. I made the treacherous passage below to check on the possibility of a repair. The electrician's mate arrived just as I did and we quickly determined it was an electrical failure. There was no possibility of repairing it in such conditions. I made my way back to the flying bridge and reported my findings to the captain. We still had the magnetic compasses. Under the circumstances, we decided they would be adequate. They had to be. But no sooner had I arrived back on the flying bridge than the lights went out without warning. We had lost all electrical power. We could be without it a few minutes but not much longer than that, not if we wanted to stay afloat.

The two auxiliary engines, which supplied us with electricity, were housed in the forward engine room and I hurried below to check on them. Others joined me, but Frye, who was on duty there, had already found the trouble and was switching us over to the other engine. When that was accomplished we checked the fuel tank for the engine that had conked out and found water in it. I had no idea how that could have happened and the thought was troubling. Frye gave me a look of incredulity. What else was taking place on the ship that we didn't know about and couldn't anticipate?

We'd been without steering for several minutes by this time. When electricity was restored the helmsman reported he had not regained power steering. In the midst of such a violent storm this was sobering news. The ship wouldn't survive the storm for long if we couldn't control her heading. By the time I got below, the switch to manual steering was being accomplished. Two of us went back to the lazarette, a small compartment on the stern of the ship accessed by lifting a deck hatch cover to check on the controlling lines. They were in good working order. The malfunction was in the steering engine itself mounted in the aft engine room. On closer examination it was determined that repair was not practical while under way. Fortunately the change to manual steering was quickly made before any adverse actions took place.

Although we had manual steering we were in serious trouble. Under the best of conditions steering such a ship without power was difficult. In the midst of a raging typhoon the task was almost insurmountable. I went to the main bridge and saw that two men were now manning the wheel, fighting with all their might to keep our bow heading directly into the waves. Not all waves were coming from the same direction. With the limited visibility caused by the driving rain and near constant spray there was very little opportunity to spot a large one. Once spotted, steering the ship manually to head her bow into it was extremely difficult and not always possible. The response time was simply too slow. Taking the waves broadside was becoming more and more disastrous. Even taking them from a quarterly direction, that is, with the bow not headed straight into one, forced the ship to change direction no matter what position the rudders were in.

We continued on our outbound course like this for an hour before Blaser decided to reverse direction and head back toward Okinawa. Coming about in such violent seas was not easy or safe. During the turn we would be vulnerable if a rogue wave, formed when two or more large waves unexpectedly joined forces, caught us broadside. Such a wave had already nearly capsized us. With the ever-increasing strength of the waves and wind the maneuver could prove to be our undoing. We had to manage the turn while in a trough between two massive waves and with only manual steering. This was daunting in the extreme.

I joined the captain and Stauffer on the flying bridge. The three of us began judging the interval of the waves. When we thought we had the longest window possible and at the moment when we were on the crest of a giant wave, Blaser shouted the order, "Full right rudder! Both engines, full speed ahead!"

We watched uneasily for the ship to respond. Long seconds, which seemed like hours, passed. Our eyes were glued to the next giant wave forming in front of us. At last the ship picked up speed and the bow began to turn ever so slowly. Did we have enough time? The wave we had been watching was now moving rapidly toward us but we were turning much faster now. The wave was rushing at us as we were broadside to it, then turned slightly away. Finally, at the last possible second, our stern was to the monster as it crashed over us. We'd done it!

Slowly, I let out my breath. I looked at Blaser and Stauffer and gave a sick grin. The captain gave orders to reduce speed to one-third, just enough to give us steerage. We were in no hurry to make the next such turn.

We were traveling with the wind and along with most of the waves now. The waves were sixty to seventy feet high and moving much faster than our ship. They came up behind us, lifted the ship into the air stern first, then worked their way along her length with a loud roar, the ship giving an awful shudder as the massive volume of water passed about her, then left her in a trough. YMS-472 was without power or steering until the waves, traveling faster than the ship, passed under her. Often another wave from a different direction caught her before power and steering had taken hold, twisting her off her course. For a long moment the screws and rudders were out of the water and the engines would race with a sickening roar.

Moving like this with the wind reduced the heavy spray but also caused the ship to yaw, making it possible for her to be swamped. Moving in this direction was worse than heading into the storm's power but both were better than being caught broadside. No direction was safe any longer. Ships far larger than our own would have trouble in such violent seas.

It is not possible to overstate how difficult steering had become. Ever since we had lost power steering two men wrestled with the sluggish wheel to maintain some control over the course of the ship. It was exhausting and imprecise.

Half an hour after reversing course I went back down to consult with my damage control crew to see if there were other problems I didn't know about. We discussed what we knew and agreed there was nothing to be done under the circumstances. I asked them to stay alert and to take up a position on the bridge so they would all be together and could act in unison if there was more trouble. Then I returned to the flying bridge. Each time I made this passage from inside I noticed the increased power of the storm. This time was no different.

I considered our situation still again and decided that our fundamental seaworthiness wasn't threatened, not yet. There was not an unusual amount of water in the bilge and the pumps were working properly. Except for the gyrocompass and power steering everything seemed to be functioning properly. The main engines were performing without a hitch and the ship's structure, despite the pounding and god-awful shuddering, appeared to be withstanding everything the storm had to give us.

Our greatest danger remained being caught broadside by a massive wave with enough power to capsize us. As long as we could head into or away from the storm the odds of that happening were reduced. What troubled me was that we were having great difficulty as it was but the storm kept growing in power.

Fate can be cruel and it was for us that day. The decision to go into the storm, then run from it, had made sense to me. I didn't see what else we could do. What we didn't know, what we had no way of knowing, was that our maneuvering kept us in the most dangerous position in the midst of the typhoon, the northeast quadrant, while the storm bore down on us from the south. Here the winds were constantly at maximum strength and it was against these powerful winds and waves that we were constantly beat in our course to and from Okinawa.

The Pacific is the largest ocean on earth. Hundreds of ships had set sail from Buckner Bay that day and each selected her own course. The odds that we would make the worst possible choices were astronomical, yet that was what we had inadvertently done, not because we were bad seamen or because our captain was remote in his dealings with us, but because it was our fate.

I had considered the possibility of suggesting we simply beach the ship on Okinawa. I was really having doubts we could survive the growing power of the storm. For some time the idea of beaching held a strong appeal to me especially as our heading took us toward the island, but finally I decided it was foolish. You don't destroy a million-dollar ship because of your concern about her ability to withstand a storm. The ship could be broken up on rocks and, anyway, there was no way to know how many of us would survive. The captain would surely have considered it as an option and it was his call.

I ran every possible alternative through my head and came up with nothing. All we could do, I told myself, was what we were doing: fight the storm, stay afloat. Still, doubts nagged my thoughts. There *must* be an answer, something else we could do, some way out of this.

Radar was giving us little help and visibility was growing worse as dusk approached. We knew from what radar did detect and by dead reckoning that we were nearing Okinawa and needed to reverse course once again. We made two more turns without incident. At 1900 that night we prepared to turn from the island a second, and what was to be our last, time.

Blaser told me he didn't want to risk another turn during the night because we wouldn't be able to see the waves to judge the maneuver. Once we were headed back out to sea we would continue on that course until dawn.

We had absolutely no sense of what was happening with the storm. We could not tell how fast it was moving, or if the worst had passed or was yet to come. Except in the most general way we did not know the direction it was traveling or what course we could take to find less violent seas. Everything that had happened since we had cleared Buckner Bay said that the storm was continuing to grow in power, and for us it was.

I went below to inform the crew of the captain's decision. Light flickered across sweaty faces as one man lit a cigarette with a trembling hand. A glance at the silent men told me they understood the necessity and had already guessed that was what we had to do. Approaching darkness and the storm gave us no choice.

Once we made that final turn and were set on our course back out to sea into the typhoon I experienced an unexpected and profound sensation of relief. There was no improvement in our situation but I was free from making any decisions. I no longer wrestled with alternatives, with the persistent thought that some answer was evading me. The die was cast. The decision was made and it was final. Whether it was right or wrong, whatever it held for us, our lot was cast.

FIVE

Capsized

Bob Hobart continued working the radio, vainly searching for some kind of contact with another ship. Maybe someone else had more information about the storm or had received new orders—anything. He established momentary contact with another ship fighting the wind and waves but lost it before any meaningful conversation took place.

A dozen men were crowded onto the small bridge, pressed against one another, feet entangled, heads lowered, every man staring straight ahead, eyes focused on nothing. One of the men lit a cigarette and the flickering light from the Zippo created an eerie shadow across the faces of the others. Another lifted a cigarette to his lips, his fingers trembling as he tried to put it in place, his hands initially unable to fumble his lighter open.

A dim-colored light came from the bulb that lit the magnetic compass dial. It cast a strange vermilion glow upon the glistening faces of the two helmsmen fighting the wheel. It was much quieter here than on the flying bridge but almost no one was talking. Occasionally one of the men spoke from barren hope, "It seems to be easing."

Each man was immersed within his own thoughts, dealing with the fear in his own way. I am certain that more than one wanted to scream, to run around the ship, tearing his clothes off, pulling at his hair, but there was nothing to be done—absolutely nothing. All of us had to take it. It no longer mattered what we wanted.

Most crew members were scarcely out of high school, only the captain was so much as thirty years old. We had been called upon to perform the duties of men and that was what we had done. Many decades later in the fullness of my years, I recall the youthful faces of that fine crew, of those wonderful boys called upon to be men, in the final terrifying hours of their life.

No matter how violent the storm, at least one man had to remain below to monitor the engines. With the watch change I cautioned Pete Hasberg to position himself on the ladder near the hatch open to the main deck so he could make a quick escape if necessary. He gave me a grin, then said, "Aye, sir," before turning to go below. The always-reliable Ash would replace him at midnight. You could set your clock by him.

I returned to the flying bridge. Blaser, Engler, and Stauffer were crouched against the bulkhead and I rushed to join them, waiting for the next wave to crash over us before rising with them. I was standing beside Stauffer. Again I experienced how much more violent the storm had grown. I cannot adequately describe the feeling of being on deck where, because of the gale, I was unable to walk except crouched over, with a vise-like grip on everything I touched. The decking was so slippery I could scarcely keep my feet down, the force of the water and wind nearly enough to take my feet from under me. The wind tore at my legs, whipping my trousers like a sail ripped free in a high wind. Volumes of water crashed onto me, stopping my movement for long moments.

There were two signal lights on the flying bridge. They also functioned as searchlights when held or locked open. The lights illuminated only the forward portion of the ship. The night beyond the tip of our ship was a black mystery. All we could see was the next wave as it crashed into us. We could hear the storm about us, the roaring sea and the howling wind out there like some terrible angry creature.

Night increased my sense of vulnerability. Out in the storm at such a time it became very personal, as if the wind and sea were directed at me alone. What I couldn't see *was* going to get me.

There were also two floodlights located on the roof of the radio room. They were directed toward the stern of the ship. They were of no practical use because we were moving into the storm and waves but gave a commanding view of the cascading water that covered the entire deck behind the superstructure where we stood. I could hardly believe we could take so much water over us and remain afloat. I felt as if our ship was becoming more like a submarine with each passing hour.

The men on the flying bridge could speak only by shouting three or four words at a time. Earlier I had spotted a place directly behind the flying bridge, between the air duct and the stairs some five feet behind Blaser, where the wall acted as a modest shield. I had no duties so I told Blaser where I'd be if there was another problem. I did not want to be trapped below.

With the diffused light coming up to us from the searchlights I could see Boyd Stauffer's face. The customary impish smile was still there but I could see it was taking a terrible effort to maintain it. Before I left the flying bridge for the last time our eyes met for a moment. I could see the strain, the fear, and the hopelessness, as I'm certain he saw the same emotions in my face. There was nothing more to say. We were beyond words. In looking back I realize that in those final seconds there was the unspoken exchange of a final farewell. I made my way down the short stairs and huddled with my back to the flying bridge. Besides my life jacket the only bit of survival gear with me was a flashlight.

The wind screamed across the guy wires that held the mast in place and wailed through the other wires, cables, and lines hanging from the yardarm. The high winds created a dissonance of high shrills, both alien and, at the same time, deafening. If one of the wires snapped loose, it would whip violently across the ship, causing destruction everywhere it struck. How long, I wondered, would they withstand this kind of fury?

If one of the guy wires broke the mast would collapse. Could the ship survive such a calamity? Would the mast drive itself through the deck or into the side of the hull, creating a gaping hole? Could my damage control team shore up the damage in these conditions and keep the ship afloat? Would it even be possible to bring the necessary timbers from below to the deck and once there could we perform the work? It was impossible. The more I listened to the shrieking of the wires the more convinced I became that the mast would surely crash down and that we could not survive if it did.

Each time the bow of the ship dove into the next massive wave the ship experienced a long, lingering shudder. When the wave crashed across us the vessel reacted with a violent shake. Once the wave reached the foredeck the ship labored as if held by a giant hand, then a solid wall of the ocean would strike the superstructure, engulfing us in black water crowned intermittently with white foam.

Every time I was amazed that our ship was still intact. If the superstructure collapsed it would have been even more catastrophic than if the mast toppled. All ability to control the ship would be lost and we would capsize in moments. Once again I wondered just how long our ship could withstand such forces. I could not imagine she had been designed to take this kind of punishment for such a long duration.

No matter how I tried my mind couldn't shake the visions I was conjuring. I recalled seeing the hull of the ship during construction. The thick reinforced wood had seemed substantial enough to me then to withstand anything. Now I wondered. Would the ship suddenly break apart? Or was it more likely she would simply give up— for that was how it seemed to me—and capsize? The fear of the unknown, of looming disaster, was almost unbearable.

The storm couldn't last forever, I reminded myself. Even now it could be moving on a course that would carry it away, or it might have spent its fury and both the wind and waves would begin to diminish. For all I knew we had already withstood the worst, that the going would get easier from here on, that this nightmare would be over by dawn, that we really would live and have a story to tell our grandchildren.

Harrison, who had so generously shared all the cigarettes he had won in New York, was on the damage control team and unexpectedly joined me. He was one of the leaders in the engine room, a friend and a man I had come to rely on very much. I'd met his pleasant, attractive wife and their two small children. I was glad to have his company.

Although sitting side by side we had to shout in short bursts to communicate over the deafening wind, crashing waves, and howling noise coming from the wind screaming across the lines of the mast. We tried to anticipate any potential damage control problems we might face. In talking about the possibilities it was as if we gained a measure of control once again. For those minutes the fear was not as great. Like alcoholics staving off the desire to drink we held our fear at bay with talk.

We talked about what to do if forced to abandon the ship. There were just the three flotation devices for all thirty-one of us in the event we were forced to abandon the ship. There was the ship's small dinghy. It could not remain afloat a single minute under these conditions. Then there were the two life rafts. Each could accommodate fourteen men in theory, although it would be very crowded. Secured on opposite sides of the ship's superstructure, I couldn't remember the last time they'd been serviced. The release latches might very well be corroded shut. And if the ship capsized only one of the rafts would be available if the ship rested on her side, neither if she turned top to bottom. The very idea of facing the storm in any of the flotation devices was unimaginable.

Harrison and I went over every scenario we could imagine and in those conditions, in the dead of night subjected to such violence, we summoned many disasters to mind. He had thought of the same on which I had already dwelled: the mast collapsing, hull failure, complete loss of steerage, loss of all power or propulsion, the collapse of the superstructure. We agreed none were imminent or necessarily inevitable. YMS-472 was proving herself a durable vessel. No, we both agreed, our greatest danger was from capsizing and few, if any, would survive such a calamity.

Even though the crew was above deck, the bridge and the other two compartments would immediately be submerged.

The men would have just seconds to somehow find a door and get it open. It would be pitch black. Water would fill the compartments in moments. There would be panic. It was unlikely anyone would manage to get out in the precious seconds of time available.

Those who did find themselves in the dark water would no longer have the protection of the ship. How could they manage to get one of the rafts free? If by some miracle they did make it into a raft, would it even be possible to remain in it? We agreed it would not. We didn't think the rafts themselves could withstand the typhoon. The ship had to survive, because we were all doomed if it did not.

Harrison was a very religious man. As he prepared to return to the bridge, leaving me alone with my thoughts, he shouted for me to hear, "God will see us through."

Now alone, I assumed a near fetal position to resist the relentless onslaught as it continued to grow in force. The ship rolled continuously to one side and then the other, only to be brought up short with a powerful wave, the whole body of the vessel rendering that awful shudder, water crashing across the ship, the wind howling, a horrible sound beyond all description.

My fear turned numb during these endless hours. What remained was a terror so profound I can scarcely express it. It filled me utterly. I knew, absolutely *knew*, the ship could not keep this up. There was no end to the storm, none! It was only a matter of time before the unthinkable happened.

I recalled an incident from my childhood. On Armistice Day, when I was in the fifth grade, we were all silently facing east at the eleventh hour. We were thinking of the many war dead and observing this moment in their memory. I wondered in my child's mind if someday I would die in a war. Would others remember me in this way at some distant date? That had been fourteen years before but at that moment in the Pacific those childhood thoughts came rushing back.

The incessant, violent wind whipped and churned the sea into a boiling cauldron. It was the wind creating these powerful waves and causing the ocean to rise and fall like moving mountains. In the darkness beyond the ship it was impossible to judge their size. Our ship's actions, however, indicated they were much higher than before, possibly as high as eighty to ninety feet. The wind whipped the rain nearly horizontally across the ship, making it very difficult to keep my eyes open even in a squint.

I was emotionally exhausted and had reached a point beyond despair. The stress, the reality of approaching oblivion on the one hand, the uncertainty of my fate on the other, was unbearable, but there was nothing to do but bear it.

I had become highly attuned to the condition of the ship and her response to the wind and towering waves. Some part of me evaluated each shudder and violent reaction of the ship. The waves came unpredictably from all directions and I knew the helmsmen were finding it impossible to know which new threat to face. We were taking more waves over both the port and starboard beams since night had fallen and the rolls of the ship were often very extreme. How long before they misjudged? How long before the ship failed to respond to the wheel and we were overwhelmed by a monster wave?

I wanted to think about anything but my impending fate. I wondered what my small family was doing at this very moment. It was about nine in the morning in Aurora, Illinois. It was early fall. I pictured Dorothy and Pat in the yard playing in the grass. Laughter. Joy. How would they manage if I never came home? How different, and more difficult, would their life be without me?

It was impossible to take my thoughts away from the storm and ship for more than a few moments. Now I recalled our final turn near Okinawa just before nightfall. I should have gone to the captain and at least told him I had been thinking about suggesting he beach the ship. Why had I assumed he had given it consideration? It was his decision to make and I had withheld information that might have caused him to make one different than he had. At this moment I would have risked beaching the ship. That would have been better than this, but all this was only so much pointless second-guessing.

Will we capsize? I kept thinking. *Are we all going to die?*

For a moment I pictured the ship breaking apart, only for that image to be replaced by one of the ship upside down in the raging sea. I saw the crew trapped below, struggling in the black water for some way out, each young man's body growing motionless as death overcame life, floating there in that limbo, trapped, until the sinking ship took them down deep into the ocean.

No thought remained with me for long. Horrible visions flashed through my mind only to be replaced by even more appalling images. There was no logic to any of it. My thoughts were beyond my control. I was exhausted, mentally and physically.

Toward midnight that night, 16 September 1945, my best estimate was that we were thirty to forty miles east of the northern tip of Okinawa. Later I found out that the center of the Makurazaki typhoon was ten miles south and fifteen miles east of the tip. The exact center of the storm was approaching and it placed us in the deadliest position possible. We were located about fifteen to twenty miles east of the eye, the point where the winds are at their maximum.

From my sheltered area I listened to the winds shriek through the tangle of wires and lines, anticipating some sign the mast was about to give away. I heard every groan of the twisted planks in the hull, experienced every shudder of the superstructure as it was struck still again by a massive wall of water. I was waiting for a telltale sound, some harbinger that something was at last giving away.

Before the storm I had known the ship intimately and had been instantly alert to the slightest change in her. Since the storm began I had become expert in reading her reaction to each new manifestation of the storm. I knew the feel of each roll, the response of the ship when she reached the farthest point in a roll, that instant of hesitation before she came back. And how she reacted if the roll was stopped by a crashing wave from the opposite direction. I had experienced these sensations a thousand times. My senses were finely honed for any change and I knew the moment the storm lessened, even the tiniest bit, I would sense it at once in the response of the ship.

So it was with sudden alarm that I realized that the ship was reacting sluggishly to the next roll. The recovery was also less precise than the one before. At first I refused to accept what my senses told me. I consciously judged the following roll and there it was—that sluggish, lethargic response. Could it be my over-active imagination? Never had my senses been keener. No, it was happening in the bow as well. When it plowed into a wave the recovering was less crisp than earlier.

Had anyone else noticed? Unlike Blaser and Stauffer, I had no duties. Here on the superstructure I was likely in the best position to first notice the change. It felt as if we were taking on sea water. Perhaps a hatch had come loose or one of the planks had ruptured. I waited for the next wave to be absolutely certain before sounding the alarm. Never have I experienced such terror.

I stood up in my small, partially sheltered area so nothing would interfere with my judgment. It was just a few steps to the captain. I took hold of the two handrails and placed my foot on the first of the four steps leading to the flying bridge just as the ship slowly, slowly, but inexorably, rolled to starboard—then continued rolling onto its side.

SIX

The Raft

The capsized ship pulled me under the water. Desperately, I clung to the handrails to avoid being swept away into the raging sea. My worst nightmare had been realized and my mind was suddenly numb with an oppressive sense of hopelessness. My body trembled as I struggled to hold onto the handrails. I was dangling in the water, unable to breathe or see, incapable of making any decision. I was in the grip of forces beyond my control and had no choice but to cling to the handrails and wait as the ship continued its roll and carried me more deeply into the black water.

As if the ship had a heart she struggled to recover from the roll, fighting to right herself as she had so many times before, but this time she failed. Despite her effort YMS-472 only partially recovered. Unexpectedly, my head suddenly broke above water. It had been nearly silent beneath the surface, now the angry cry of the wind whipped my ears. In a series of coughs and gasps I spit out the sea water I had taken into my mouth and nose, then sucked great gulps of air into my lungs. I tried frantically to clear my head. I had to think. I had to plan. It wasn't just my life but that of the others onboard depending on me. The sky was black as ink, great walls of water crashed down on the ship. I hung onto the handrails with a vice grip, knowing my life depended on it. If I was swept away into the storm all was lost.

That final fatal roll had not seemed as serious as the ones before so it came as a shock when it was the last. Poised to rush to the captain I had thought there would be time to take some action, determine the problem, and implement a solution. The suddenness of the ship's failure had been stunning. We had surely capsized because something below deck had gone terribly wrong and we had taken on sea water. It made no difference now.

The ship nosed into the ocean as she capsized. When she returned just slightly she lay on her starboard side with her bow buried in the water. The generator was within a watertight room and from the depths of the dark water, light from the ship partially lit the area about me, casting a curious azure hue.

Out of the darkness a wave struck with such force that my hands were wrenched from their hold on the handrails. I landed hard on the exposed side of the chart room, which was now the deck. YMS-472, my home for nearly a year, a ship whose every sound and crevice I had come to know like the backyard in which I had grown up, lay mortally stricken in the angry seas—and was sinking. Along with my fear was another emotion, difficult if not impossible to describe. It would have been the same if a cyclone had torn my parents' house out by its foundation and lifted it off into the sky for destruction before my eyes.

The ship had also been my only hope for surviving the storm. I'd already decided survival was impossible in one of the life rafts or wearing just a life jacket. But now I had no choice. I could see the port side raft ten or fifteen feet from where I lay. The other one was under water. The port raft was completely exposed, strapped in its cradle by Y-shaped canvas straps. A pelican hook, held in place by a metal ring, had a release lever. I crawled through the howling wind and smashing waves to the latch. I tried to release it so the raft would come free but it wouldn't budge. The latch was corroded in place. I beat on it with my fists, pulled and pushed at it, even tried to kick it, all without results.

Niles McQueen, an electrician's mate, crawled up and joined me at the raft. I'd last seen him on the bridge. I knew he had a knife because his duties called for one. He wore it hanging from his belt along with a ring of keys. "Niles! Do you have your knife?" I shouted into the wind. "I can't get the latch open! We've got to cut the belt!" McQueen fumbled at his side, then cut through the strap near him. He handed the knife to me to cut the other strap. Now the raft was only resting in its cradle. "Let's lift it out and set it over here!" I shouted. The two of us reached down, pulled the raft out, and placed it on the side of the exposed hull. Then we waited for others to join us.

The only portion of the superstructure that offered immediate escape to those trapped inside the ship was the bridge and the door to the bridge located just a few feet away. Men were joining us, coming out of that doorway, crawling, braced against the wind and waves. To exit the chart room or the radio room the crew trapped there had to first make their way onto the bridge. In a suddenly clear mind I realized what was taking place this very moment just a few feet away through the walls of the superstructure.

With the ship lying on its side, water was rapidly entering her rooms. The bridge had been lit only by the red glow from the magnetic compass. The other crowded rooms were utterly dark and that bit of red light was insufficient to serve as a beacon for the panicked men. In the chaos they were struggling to find air, locate the passageway, and make their way out. They had only seconds. Frye was in there. So was Hobart. So many shipmates, so many friends. There was a life and death struggle taking place right now. In a few short moments it would be over. Each man trapped inside would at some instant draw sea water instead of air into his lungs. The only immediate survivors were going to be the handful of men who made it to this single raft in the next few minutes.

I didn't realize it until much later that almost immediately after the ship capsized the outer edge of the eye of the typhoon passed over us. The center of the eye was approximately twenty to thirty miles west of our location when we capsized at about 0100 on 17 September 1945. There was no letup in the violence of the ocean, which beat at us unmercifully, but for a few moments the wind suddenly diminished. It was easier to move about, not such a struggle to be heard.

Three men joined McQueen and me: Freeman Hetzer, Bob Hicks, and Harold Perry. Reaching the raft, George Casleton shouted, "Some are still coming from the bridge." Upon arriving, Bill Harrison said, "I got out of the bridge. I think more are coming." *Good,* I thought, *that's good. Maybe all of us will get away after all.*

Just then Lester Talley crawled toward us from the bridge doorway. I could see what he was about to do and opened my mouth to shout. Before I could and without a word or order he pushed the raft into the water. I was caught completely by surprise. I had assumed we would keep the raft on the ship so it would not drift away as we gathered survivors. Now it was in the turbulent water without a tether. In seconds it would be swept away and we would be left to go down with the ship. All of us leaped into the roiling water and swam to the side of the raft.

The raft was a rectangle, nine by four and a half feet. The flotation portion was a nine-inch square ring of balsa wood wrapped in gray canvas. Secured to it was a rope netting. Attached to that was a flooring of wood lattice that held the survival equipment and provisions.

The raft was hugging the ship's keel with the action of the waves moving it, and us, along the ship's hull toward the stern. "The engines may be running!" I shouted. "The screws might still be turning. We have to push away from the hull before we get chewed up!"

We all took a firm grasp on the outer ring of the raft. With our feet and hands we pushed it away from the ship. The ship also had a number of depth charges that could be set to "safe" or to explode at various depth settings. Normally when in a harbor or bay, regulations called for the safe setting. However, even though we had been in a bay for a few days, we thought possibly and inadvertently they may not have been set on safe. We feared they would explode when they reached specified depth settings. "We need to get as far from the ship as possible!" I shouted. Everyone understood the danger and hand-paddled furiously to move the raft a safe distance from the ship. The waves were still moving us toward the stern of the ship. We pushed ourselves away from the hull, swimming and pushing the raft ahead of us to clear the stern of the ship at a safe distance.

Bill Ash suddenly appeared in the water nearby. His instructions had been to remain at the foot of the ladder in the engine room so he could make his escape in case we capsized and here he was. I was glad to see him but he was the last to reach the life raft. Of the thirty-one aboard, just nine of us clung to the balsa wood rim with our bodies dangling in the water, fighting to keep from being torn away and cast adrift. This life raft was our only hope. I doubted anyone left to the elements in a life jacket could last the night in these turbulent conditions. I had my doubts the raft would survive the pounding but there was no alternative.

The captain was gone, as was Engler. So was my friend Boyd Stauffer. They had been tossed into the water from the flying bridge and had probably been quickly separated from the ship. They were likely still alive at this moment, calling out, flailing their arms in the water, trying to swim toward the ship, desperate to locate the raft. How long could they last?

No one else was in sight. We shouted, calling out repeatedly, trying to make enough noise so anyone in the water hearing us could make it to the raft. Water washed over us continuously and we were constantly coughing and spitting out sea water. With my flashlight I signaled into the storm but its feeble light had no effect on the dark. No one came.

A few minutes after the ship had partially righted herself, the lights abruptly blinked out. YMS-472 was lost to the darkness. Water had obviously finally reached the generator. I didn't see my ship go down but she could not have stayed afloat much longer. It was just as well. I had no desire to see her die.

With the loss of artificial light the night turned even blacker. In all my life I have never since experienced such complete darkness. I could see absolutely nothing—not the white foam on the roiling water, not the raft to which I clung, not any of my shipmates. It was darkness as complete and profound as is possible. My world existed now only in sound and touch.

Despite no letup in the crashing waves, the wind was not as violent as just a few minutes ago so the men climbed onto the raft and tried to sit on the outer ring. Joining them, I was suddenly filled with calm. My greatest fear had taken place and I had survived. I experienced a profound sense of relief. My fate was decided. This realization eased from me the terror with which I had been filled during this long, dreadful night, the worst night of my life.

Although an outlandish thought given our situation, I experienced hope for the first time in many hours. Perhaps the body can take only so much of fear, so many agonizing hours of terror, before it needs respite, some release from hopelessness. I don't know. But sitting on the edge of the raft, having survived my greatest fear—the capsizing of my ship—I began to think it possible that I might again see my wife and daughter.

Without warning the wind suddenly restored to its full fury. The eye of the typhoon had passed and we were back in the maelstrom, only now we were in the water without the protection our ship had given us. We rose on a mountain of water. At the crest, without warning, the wind lifted the raft with the nine of us onboard like a gust of autumn wind might toss a leaf across the yard. We were thrown into the air, then crashing into the water. As we came to the surface and drew a breath of air we shouted to one another in the blackness and swam back against the waves to cling again to the outside of the raft. My rain boots and pants had nearly pulled me under so I hurriedly stripped them off. All I now wore was my rain jacket, shirt, pants, and life jacket.

Without light, there was no warning when each powerful wave crashed over us. They came out of the dark like a solid wall and buried us beneath a mass of water, spitting and sputtering for air as each finally passed, until seconds later when the next one landed. In those moments the rain whipped into us, each drop striking like the sting of a wasp. We kept our eyes closed against the raindrops but opened them again and again as we tried to see one another, tried to see the waves and anticipate when the next giant one would strike. There was no relief, no release from the shrieking wind and pounding water, no escape from our anxiety and gnawing fear.

Conversation was impossible. Sea water was in our eyes, mouths, and throats. We coughed and choked constantly. We could scarcely breathe, even at the least violent moments. By our nature and training we sought to work as a team, but the elements and our circumstances worked against us. For all our desire and efforts to look out for one another, this was very much a personal battle. Each of us fought alone, each of us dealt with his panic and fear in his own way. Our instincts and our desire for self-preservation drove us. Our movements were without thought. They were in immediate response to what was happening that second.

We were constantly shouting to one another to make certain none of us had been swept away. When the most violent of the waves crashed over us, pulling us from the side of the raft until we could struggle back, we did head counts, trying our best to be certain all nine of us were still there. We found it impossible to get an accurate count under such conditions because some men inevitably answered more than once.

"Is everyone here?" I shouted after I had managed to get back to the raft after being thrown into the water the fourth time. I heard a scattering of replies that gave me no assurance that all of the men were at the raft. "I'm assigning numbers," I shouted. "Answer with your number from now on! Talley your number is one! Harrison yours is two!"

Giving each man a number was not easy because not everyone could hear me at any one time. They were passing information to each other at the same time as I was trying to give every man his number. With the deafening wind and constant waves it took some time before I was satisfied everyone knew his number. The next time we were lifted and thrown into the water, I made my way back to the raft. The number system immediately broke down. It was pandemonium and all of us were gripped with fear, obstructing logical thinking. Also, Hicks, Hetzer, and Harrison each started with an H and more than one often answered when another's name was called. Some men were confused or didn't understand what I was trying to do or had forgotten and answered with his name. Then Hetzer responded with both his name and number. The process was never complete, never fully realized. It was chaos, as confusing and unreliable as simply shouting out our names had been.

Quite simply, conditions were too violent to allow us any order. In addition, each one of us was terrified. We all knew that at every moment we were within seconds of drowning. We had lost our ship. Although battered, she had given us some measure of assurance. If the storm could sink our ship, how long could any of us expect to survive hanging onto a balsa wood raft? The words didn't have to be uttered. We all knew the reality of our desperate situation.

The ocean was a churning mass that constantly tore at us from all directions. The black sky and water prevented any sense of proportion. The experience was suffocating. The wind repeatedly tossed the raft, and us, about like a child's toy. No matter if we looked up or down, right or left, the wind whipped stinging spray and rain against our exposed faces, from every direction.

Every few moments winds of special fury struck and toppled the raft, casting us off like so many rag dolls. We had no warning, no means of preparing ourselves. Once again we would be adrift in the vast ocean, gasping for air, searching for the raft, floundering in the raging water, our arms flailing, instinctively struggling to get back to that last bit of hope. We could not see each other or the raft. Each time we were tossed away there was a furious scramble to establish contact with the raft and one another. Whenever someone reached the raft he would scream, "Here it is!" at the top of his voice, again and again. We'd follow that voice through the roaring wind, joined by others until we reached the edge of the raft.

There was no time to worry about what was taking place. Within seconds we'd be struck again, shouting one more time to be certain no one was separated from the raft, sputtering, coughing, and hacking in the water. We clung to the edge of the raft with all our strength, coping every instant with our panic.

During that long night there was not a moment's respite from the wind and waves. We were in continuous struggle, growing more exhausted with each passing hour, the water and the wind constantly pulling us away, seeking to wrench us from the raft. Had we not been young men, in the prime of life, none of us would have survived.

Words cannot adequately describe what I cannot convey with sufficient force—the shear, unrelenting terror of those devastating, long hours. Take the most frightening instant of your life, magnify it a thousand times, then extend it without letup through the snail-like passing of the longest, blackest night of your life, and you begin to approach what it was like. Add exhaustion such as you've never known, horrible sensations, and powerful, alien forces constantly bludgeoning you— forces that you've never before experienced—and perhaps you have the slightest inkling of what we suffered. If ever there was a more terrible punishment, I don't know what it is.

There was no end to it, there was never a letup. Neither the wind nor the overwhelming waves were diminished as we fought to stay alive. The water slapped at us when it didn't submerge us and we spit out salt water from our nose and mouth, struggling to keep our lungs clear. It was the most exhausting experience of my life.

After a time we gave up taking head counts. We were simply too spent from our struggle to make the effort. It was all each of us could do to cling to the raft, to make our way back to it when torn away, only to cling to it again for a moment's respite before it began again. Each of us feared being unable to find the raft. Upon reaching it we feared finding it destroyed by the violence and force of the storm. Without the raft and its supplies we stood no chance of survival. Each time we were flung into the raging sea, every time we fought our way back, we were in the grip of the persistent fear that our last refuge, the raft, would be gone, or that we would be unable to find it. It was enough to drive any of us insane and I have no doubt that more than one of us had periods of incoherence that dreadful night. The truth, our reality, was more than we could bear.

I have often thought of that night, of the struggle to remain with the raft, to stay afloat—to endure. To survive that typhoon in our state was surely as close to a miracle as there has ever been.

I've often considered the human body and its reaction when exposed to the prospect of death. Not just its physical capabilities but also the mental, how they function in concert for survival. I know no matter how weary I became, or how many times I was thrown from the raft, or how often I was submerged and fought my way back, I never once gave any thought to giving up. I fought the raging storm on the open sea. Waves eighty to ninety feet tall, winds well over one hundred miles an hour, blown from the crests of massive waves, struggling my way repeatedly out of the black water to gasp in a breath of air, only to be slapped in the face. Then pounded by yet another giant wave. No matter how difficult it was, how impossible our situation seemed, I instinctively did everything I could to stay alive.

My body reacted without any thought or logical consideration on my part. It did what it had to do. In the darkest of moments when survival is at stake, the mind blocks from us any thought about the possibility of not surviving and directs the body's instinctive response. Time and again I intuitively made the right choice and marveled to find myself back with the raft and my shipmates. I had not consciously thought to cling to the handrails when the ship capsized. I just did. When I was repeatedly thrown from the raft I always struggled to the water's surface and found my way back to it. This was repeated so many times that I could not even begin to estimate them. It was endless. My body and mind did what was necessary to keep me alive.

Although much that was horrible followed, that night and its memory have never left me for a second. In its own way, the night in the open water during a horrendous typhoon seared an even deeper mark upon me than what was to come.

As the long hours passed, my fatigue grew more profound. I was enveloped in a cloak of black, assaulted by ceaseless powerful forces. I struggled with less energy, fighting the wind and waves with increasing lassitude. My fear was so pronounced, so all encompassing, it ate at my core like a powerful acid, eroding my self-confidence, destroying hope. Slowly, that pervasive sense of doom, which had overwhelmed me aboard the ship, returned. How long could I survive a storm that would never end?

Could I live long enough to see the dawn?

Elmer Renner in Panama, March 1944.

Commissioning of YMS-472, 10 November 1944.*U.S. Navy*

Crew of YMS-472 at commissioning, 10 November 1944. *U.S. Navy*

YMS-472 exiting St. Johns River, heading for open sea to conduct sea trials, November 1944. Note the raft mounted on side of ship at approximately midship. *U.S. Navy*

YMS-472 heading out to sea, November 1944. *U.S. Navy*

YMS-472 and YMS-454 crews, with their dates, at USO party prior to leaving for the Pacific, 1 June 1945. *USO*

Elmer Renner with his wife, Dorothy, and nine-month-old daughter Pat, March 1945.

Edward Hicks at the wheel during the trip to Hawaii, August 1945.
Note the inclinometer mounted on the overhead. Hicks was lost
when YMS-472 capsized in the Makurazaki typhoon.

Robert Hicks, April 1945.
Freeman Hetzer, April 1945.

Bill Harrison, April 1945.

The many guy wires and lines of YMS-472's mast.

Elmer Renner

Bruce Gouldsberry

Part Two

ADRIFT

SEVEN

Dawn

After an eternity passed, followed by another, then another, long after I was no longer capable of coherent thought, when my struggle had become rote, when my energy had ebbed to its final reserves, I knew beyond any doubt, this night would never end. I was fated to die amid the crashing waves and howling wind. Only then did the faintest of glimmers, dull and distant, penetrate the black clouds ever so slightly. When I realized I was seeing the dawn my numbed mind grasped that the night was ending.

You can make it! I thought. *You can make it!*

The murky light of the fore dawn ever so slowly eased through the black of that endless night, scarcely discernible through the thick, low hanging clouds that seemed to reach down to the crests of the still raging monstrous waves. Yet it was hope; it was salvation.

A typhoon, especially over water, is not at all like a thunder-storm, which moves across the face of land. When a thunder-storm passes the sun reappears and all is calm with very little, if any, residual effect from the storm. A typhoon is immense, covering thousands of square miles, possessing enormous energy, traveling uninterrupted and slowly over vast reaches of deep water, and creating waves of incredible magnitude and force. With nothing but open water there are no obstacles to impede the waves so they persist long after the wind dissipates or moves on. They work off their fury only slowly, as dangerous in dying as they were at birth.

When the meager light had grown enough to allow me to see the water it was nothing short of terrifying. I was one of nine men clinging to the outer perimeter of our small raft. We were struggling every second to maintain our grip, subject to the violence of the wind and water each moment. The mountainous waves were cresting and the wind swept from them huge sheets of water, taking us along when we found ourselves on the peak. Again we were thrown clear of the raft. Still again we struggled against the water to make our way back. Once again we did a head count to be certain we had all made it.

The only improvement in our situation was that we now could predict when we would be thrown into the tempest. We could see the waves coming. Although no matter how tightly we held onto the raft, the wind and the waves were too powerful for us. We now could find our way back with more certainty but our own helplessness in the face of such forces was only increased by what we were not yet able to see.

As morning slowly came I realized that although the shrieking wind remained violent it was not quite as powerful as it had been. What every soul aboard YMS-472 had prayed for throughout the night had finally come to pass.

The storm was moving away from us, reluctantly releasing us from its grip.

Something else happened to me with the coming of daylight. I realized that we had survived the worst. *You've made it!* I thought. *You've made it!*

None of us was far away from the other and I could just make out the faces of my fellow shipmates. Here were my friends Harrison, Hetzer, and Ash. Young Perry had made it as had Hicks, Talley, Casleton, and McQueen. Every one of us was exhausted and our continuing struggle against the storm required our final reserves. We were bone weary to a degree I cannot explain, at a state of utter exhaustion. The merciless pounding, the scream of the wind, the endless fears and anxiety, compounded by unknown threats, had numbed our minds. We were incapable of intelligent thought, unable to communicate in any normal fashion, each wrapped within the shell of his own body.

I believe we survived only because that accursed night finally passed. If it had continued another hour, not one of us would still have been alive to see the dawn. The light was growing and I let myself imagine for a moment that the waves were not quite as tall as earlier.

I believe every one of us on the small ring of balsa wood had come to believe in his own insignificance by this time. Our raft was the tiniest spot in the vastness of that immense ocean. That and the enormity of the storm created a sense of helplessness and irrelevance in each of us.

Instinctively, I knew that was wrong. Fate, or the hand of God, had touched each one of us or we would not now be alive. Had I hesitated on the ship in the place where I crouched and decided to wait one more roll before climbing to the flying

bridge I would have been thrown free of the ship when it capsized and certainly drowned. Had I left just a few seconds
sooner I would have been on the flying bridge and would have
suffered the same fate as Blaser, Stauffer, and Engler. Only
because we rolled over at the instant my hands gripped the ladder, and because I managed to hold on like a vise, was I able to
stay with the ship. Only because I remained with the ship had I
made it to the raft. But what if McQueen had never reached the
raft in those few moments after the ship partially recovered? He
was one of the few crewmen with a knife and the only one to
reach the raft with one. Without the knife we would never have
freed the raft and none of us would have survived.

I forced myself to concentrate on the others. No one
appeared to have suffered any serious injury during the night.
Even though we could now see the hostile environment that
assaulted us no one appeared on the verge of surrender despite
looking like we were ready to collapse from exhaustion. As we
began at last to speak to one another, it became clearer that
both the wind and waves were now less powerful. Morale was
better than I had a right to expect. We were still thrown from
the raft but less frequently and each return to it was less ardu-
ous than the last.

There was, I allowed myself to think, every reason for hope.
With the severity of the typhoon it was unlikely we had been
the only ship to capsize given the hundreds that had moved out
to sea. Many of us would not be reporting back in. The
moment the storm allowed, planes and ships would begin
searching for us. We had the advantage of having floundered
relatively close to land rather than well out to sea so the air
search would be more intensive than it might otherwise have
been. We had water, food, a signal gun, and other survival items

on our well-equipped raft. We would be able to summon a plane or ship once one was in sight. There was, I believed, no reason not to be optimistic.

As we swam back to the raft after having been thrown from it again, when the light was stronger than before, one of the men shouted, "The bottom's gone! It's gone!" With a sinking heart I saw it was true.

The raft was constructed a bit like an accordion. First, the rectangular ring to which we clung held the entire raft afloat. Next, a netting of three-eighth-inch ropes secured the flotation ring to the final piece of the accordion, the wooden lattice flooring. All provisions—food, water, oars, signal gun, medical supplies, absolutely everything we needed to survive—had been strapped to the floor. Each of us saw that the floor was now gone.

Aboard the ship I had questioned whether the raft could survive the power of the storm and had been partially right in my assessment that it could not. The violent, turbulent action of the waves and wind incessantly pounding against the raft had at some point during the night torn away the floor. The only reminder that it had ever existed was some rope netting dangling in the water. All that remained to us was this small ring of balsa wood.

The loss of our supplies was a terrible blow. Knowing there would be provisions had given us confidence that the nightmare was over and that we would survive. Now that was gone! Because we were still fighting the storm and struggling to stay alive, the full realization of our fate didn't come to us until much later.

By midmorning we were being thrown from the raft much less often. The wind calmed further and the waves were noticeably less powerful although still very imposing and threatening. The times when we were pitched from the raft were now infrequent enough that we climbed aboard the ring and sat on it with our feet dangling in the water. With daylight we could anticipate the next upset and prepare ourselves accordingly. The periods atop the balsa wood increased with each passing hour. We now had time to consider and discuss our plight. We talked primarily about the loss of our provisions, which we all took very hard.

Because we spent so much time in the ocean and were thrown into it with such violence, it had been impossible for us not to swallow sea water. I had made a conscious effort not to but had still taken in some. At the diesel school at Penn State University I had read Eddie Rickenbacker's 1943 *Seven Came Through* about survival in the Pacific. The famed World War I ace and race car driver had been shot down over the Pacific while flying a B-17 bomber. He had survived, along with others, thirty days adrift. I recalled what he had said about the debilitating effects of drinking sea water and I cautioned everyone about it. When water got into their mouths I told them to be certain they spit it out. I know some men ignored my advice.

Normal conversation was now possible. After we absorbed the impact of the loss of our provisions we rationalized that our situation was not as serious as we first feared. We were certain we would be spotted and rescued no later than the following day. We knew the storm had to ease even more before the military would risk planes and the waves were still high enough that it was unlikely any ship could spot us at this time. We resigned ourselves to waiting.

Talking among ourselves we became certain that during the early evening hours of the previous night Hobart had made radio contact with other ships and advised them of our intended maneuvering plans. At the time it had seemed to me he was establishing no meaningful contact with any of the other ships but now I was not so certain. As a result we were still upbeat about our situation, especially as the winds continued to calm and the size and frequency of the waves diminished. Hunger and thirst had not as yet begun to have any effect. We were still too excited about being alive that one more day was not going to be a problem.

We took inventory of what supplies each of us carried. I had the flashlight I'd used to try and signal our location to others immediately after the ship capsized. McQueen had his knife. Ash carried a pair of pliers and one of the other men had a piece of string some thirty inches long. That was the sum and substance of our entire survival gear other than the life jackets and clothing each of us wore. It surely didn't seem like much, and it wasn't. I took it as a good sign that no one was injured during the capsizing or the ensuring aftermath. Everyone was whole and even with the realization that our survival supplies were gone we were in relatively good spirits. We were all quite certain that without a doubt we would be rescued the next day. Our comments were optimistic. Because we had survived we supposed that others had as well, without facing the harsh reality that such an assumption meant. We were convinced some of our shipmates had managed to escape the ship and were floating in the water with their life jackets. We were confident they would be found, just as we knew that we would be. We talked primarily about our situation and expressed concern for the others floating out there.

Seven of the nine on the raft had been on the main bridge. This made sense because the bridge had a doorway that opened directly onto the left side of the ship that was above water. We convinced ourselves that it was likely others on the bridge made it out after Talley pushed the raft into the water.

We talked about Blaser, Stauffer, and Engler. The final roll had not been especially violent and we convinced ourselves to believe they had not been thrown far from the ship. In the night and amid the violence of the storm I had given them up for lost. Now I was not so certain. At the moment I had risen out of the water with my hands gripping the ladder they could have been close together and not far away. Whatever fate they had suffered, or were now to face, I had been spared despite being just a few feet from them when the ship capsized.

I couldn't imagine they had sustained any injuries as a result of the capsizing unless somehow they had been thrown against some portion of the ship and been rendered unconscious. The wind and waves had in all likelihood moved them in the same general course that had carried us so they ought not be far away.

From time to time one of us would shout out for others, hoping to attract them to the sound of our voice. We all did this on occasion, hoping there would be a response from someone. There never was. Yet we were certain shipmates had to be close by and we wouldn't give up trying to gain their attention. It was difficult to view anything on the water because the waves were still too high for us to see any distance. Also, the clothing we wore and our life jackets were gray, very similar to the color of the water.

What had happened to Albert, our coati mundi, I wondered. The monkey someone had brought onboard had proved a mistake and we had given him away while we were docked in San Pedro. Cat had jumped ship at Pearl Harbor. Then the parakeet had flown away, leaving only Albert, the coati mundi. I had passed many peaceful hours with him nestled in my arms as I stood watch. I had seen Albert at midday the previous afternoon on the bridge, seeking shelter in a cabinet, quivering in a tight ball of fear. I never saw him again.

I had time now to think coherently and ponder our situation. My thoughts turned to the capsizing. When I was sitting in my slightly protected area behind the flying bridge, I had been certain that just before we took the final roll, something was wrong with the ship. Reliving it in my mind I was convinced we had taken on water in the bow. There had been a definite sluggishness in the way the bow had been acting. Normally when taking a frontal wave, the bow would quickly respond by lifting itself up out of the water as the wave passed. Instead, it had stayed down much longer. When it did come up, it didn't rise as far as usual. I had felt the difference.

How, I wondered, had water entered the hold? All the forward compartments were watertight and the only access to them was through other watertight compartments. One answer was that we had suffered a partial hull failure. Knowing the thickness of the hull planks, having seen them during construction, and the soundness with which they were assembled, I found that hard to accept. The only other possibility was that the pivot joint for the boom we used for sweeping acoustic mines had been damaged. It was mounted and pivoted on the bow just above the water line. Maybe the pivot joint failed. Perhaps during the violent night, with the waves tearing at it, the joint had finally wrenched free, creating a hole for the water to enter the anchor chain locker. I knew I would never know for a fact what had happened but it had to have been one of these two possibilities.

As the storm continued to abate, tension eased among the men. Talk now became more continuous and discussion broke into groups on occasion. The men talked about the method of our eventual rescue. Would we be seen by another ship or would a plane spot us and pass along the word?

Our thinking remained positive. We were convinced that we would be picked up on the next day or, at worse, the day after. We knew we were still close to Okinawa, and within easy reach of a rescue effort. The rain had stopped and visibility was improved. Only the sea, which still rose and fell, was creating a mist that limited our sight to perhaps one thousand yards. Because of our hope for rescue, even though it was unlikely this soon after the typhoon had passed, we scanned the horizon around us constantly. We all sat on the ring of the raft. I finally removed my rain jacket, leaving me clothed in pants, shirt, and a life jacket. It was cool but not cold so I wasn't uncomfortable.

Conversation dwindled off as slowly each of us drew within himself. I think most of the men were praying, just as I was. I thought of Dorothy, Pat, and my parents as well. This time, however, my thoughts were upbeat because I was certain I would see all of them again. It was only a matter of time and patience. I was very thankful I had survived the entire ordeal— or so I thought. What none of us knew was that the worst lay ahead.

I looked at each of the men in turn. I had earlier been re- lieved to see a friend and one of my crew from the engine room, Bill Harrison, from Whittier, California. It now seemed a lifetime ago that we had planned to resume our work on the ship's evaporator. He had a wife and two small boys. I was glad for them that he had survived.

There was Bill Ash from Connecticut, another one of my engineering crew. He too had a young wife. He and Harrison were good friends, Ash being the quieter of the pair. Of all the young men aboard the ship Ash was the most serious-minded.

Young Hal Perry was with us, perhaps the smallest survivor. He was no older than eighteen. Also from Connecticut, I recalled for a moment his single mom. She would be receiving that dreaded telegram. Although wounded in Normandy, Hal had survived. He'd survived again. Amazing! I thought some people were just born lucky.

There was Bob Hicks, another young crewman, quite ordinary. He was from Alabama and had always struck me as being a little shy. Looking at him now there was nothing to distinguish him from so many of the crew.

Niles McQueen from Louisiana had made it. He was somewhat of a loner and had a tendency to react without thought in critical situations. Luckily it was probably his instinctive reaction to the capsizing that allowed him to get out of the bridge as quickly as he did. If he hadn't joined me by the raft with his knife, it was unlikely any of us would have survived.

Freeman Hetzer was also on the raft. He was tall and lean, just twenty years old. I knew him the least of anyone aboard ship, primarily because he served on the deck crew. He played an awkward but energetic brand of basketball.

George Casleton, nineteen or twenty years old, was a member of my engine room gang. A ladies man from Chicago originally, he had joined us in San Pedro. Likable and ambitious, what I recall best about him was his willingness to pitch in and do his part even if the task was unpleasant.

Les Talley was infamous for putting the ship into reverse at exactly the wrong time. He was the ship's clown, a bit round in build, a practical jokester. I remember him bursting into the officers' mess, chasing the steward's mate with a butcher knife. How many men were dead, I wondered, because he'd thrown the raft into the raging water without waiting for others to join us?

There it was. God, the hand of fate, whatever you want to call it, had selected these eight plus myself for salvation. Why these and not others? I wondered if there was a purpose in their survival or if the selection had been nothing more than random chance, a product of luck and the caprice of the storm?

Late that morning Perry shouted, "Hey! Look over there! See that orange thing? It looks like one of our floats!"

"Yeah, I see it," Casleton said. "Wait a minute, it dropped into a trough. There it is! See it?" The object was thirty or forty yards away.

Harrison said, "Let's paddle to it, see if there's something else with it."

"Look!" Ash said, "there's something floating there."

"Good," I answered them all. "Maybe there are other things we can find. We must have been floating in the same direction during the night. Keep on looking. Maybe we can spot the captain or Stauffer, or anybody who might have made it off the ship."

Harrison said, "I know Frye was right next to me on the bridge. I think he got out too."

Then Perry said, "Those look like a couple of onions floating over there. Let's get them."

"I'll swim for them," McQueen said.

"No, wait a minute," I said. I didn't want anyone going off on their own. "We can paddle the raft closer."

Harrison shouted. "Anybody out there? We're over here! Anybody, yell out. Frye! You out there! Can you hear me!"

We listened. Nothing.

We continued paddling and reached the onions. "You guys divide them up," I said. "I don't want any." Most of the men took a portion, which they quickly consumed. We resumed paddling toward the orange object.

Perry spoke next. "Look right in front of us. I think that's flooring from the flying bridge."

He was right. It was a piece of lattice wood flooring of the type from the deck of the flying bridge. It was gray like the sea and that was the reason we had not spotted it previously even though it was much closer to us than the brightly colored buoy. We tore strips two or three feet long from it thinking to use them as paddles but they were so thin they proved useless.

Paddling with our hands and the worthless wood strips, we slowly and very clumsily moved toward what proved to be a marker buoy. There were no special markings on it but it was of the type carried on minesweepers to designate areas known to be mined. Driven by identical winds and waves it had traveled along the same route.

We found no other debris of any kind. With all the material onboard the ship that could have floated free I was surprised we found so little, but then the waves were still high enough and the mist so thick that we couldn't really see for much distance.

From time to time one of the men would call out. "Anyone out there? We're over here!" There were no answers. One of the crew would occasionally call out the name of a friend. But it was always the same.

For my part I scanned the water around us constantly, looking for any sign of the three men who had been on the flying bridge. I just knew they were drifting not far away. If this flotsam had remained so close to us, why not them? They had been standing on the very lattice we had found floating near us. From where I was, however, with the waves and sea rising and falling, with the mist, it simply wasn't possible to see any distance and I spotted nothing.

As time passed with no sign of anyone else I began to lose confidence that there were other survivors. Earlier I had assumed some of the crew had managed to escape the ship's sinking in addition to the three men on the flying bridge. Not being able to find anyone, when I knew they had to be close by if they had survived, it slowly came to me that we alone—nine of thirty-one—had survived. Twenty-two had not made it, nineteen of them may have been trapped inside the ship.

I found myself visualizing the panic-stricken struggle that had happened within the ship compartments as water began pouring in. It would not have been a case of water seeping in slowly. It would have gushed in as the entire starboard side of the ship was suddenly submerged. The compartments would have been pitch black. With the ship lying on its side, disorientation would have been likely among the men crowded into the cramped space. The communications equipment in the radio shack would have tumbled from the mounts into the narrow aisle and fallen on top of the men.

There was only one small, narrow door leading onto the main bridge. It was the one and only escape route. I could see the mass of humanity, fumbling with the dislodged equipment, arms flailing, legs kicking and struggling against the in-rushing torrent of sea water, as each man desperately tried to free himself and find the way out, knowing each second counted. As the water surged in, I could imagine it quickly filling the compartments, eroding the initial panic, and replacing it almost at once with hopelessness.

Men trapped inside a compartment would have held their breath for as long as they could, realizing even as they did the finality of it all. Yet they would try to keep the water from entering their lungs as long as possible as they struggled in a vain search to find another breath of air to keep them alive. Finally, unable to restrain themselves their last breaths would have been of sea water, drawn into their lungs, coughed out, drawn in again, then slowly they would have submitted to unconsciousness. The frantic flailing of their arms and legs would slowly give way, their bodies grown limp. They finally would have floated to the top of the compartment and then been carried into the depths of the sea by the sinking ship.

To describe those final awful moments is to make it impersonal, to strip it of all emotion. Yet I put a face on those figures floating in their eternal tomb. They were my shipmates, my friends. On a small ship such as YMS-472 we lived in close quarters, spent many hours on watch together, and came to know one another very personally. I had met many of their family members and sweethearts. During the long lonely midnight to 0400 watch we talked of our past and of our future plans and dreams. The men were young, most no older than nineteen or twenty years of age. Only five were married. Of the officers, three of us were married, each with children. The war was over, and during the past month every one of those men had looked forward to returning to their lives at home. We had been like one large family.

As the day passed and I saw no sign of other survivors I slowly accepted that only the nine on this remnant of a raft were all that remained. The others were gone, their lifeless bodies adrift in the sea or below in the ship that had become their grave.

There are no words to adequately describe the loss of twenty-two close friends. My emotions were tearing at me, taking me first one direction then another. My future, the future of all of us on that raft, seemed secure and I should have been exuberant, but I wasn't. Whenever I experienced the slightest sense of elation at my own good fortune the sobering vision of that final struggle within the ship came to life. I could see the expressions on their faces as they drew their last breaths. I wondered what their final thoughts had been. Or was there any thinking at all? Had the body's reaction to the struggle shut out any mental process at that last instant?

Their loss left me dejected and depressed. As I sat on the rim of the raft, balancing myself against the motion of the still tumultuous sea, I was facing outward from the center with my legs dangling in the water, my elbows on my knees, my cupped hands supporting my head. I looked down into the water but saw nothing except the faces on those motionless bodies. I sat there in a daze, unable to think of anything but the loss of so many shipmates and friends.

Some were sitting as I was. Others were hanging on the ring with their arms, their bodies suspended in the water. Little was being said. Perhaps we were all thinking the same thing. I don't know. Maybe most of them were praying. I know many of us did a great deal of praying.

The seas calmed significantly and each of us sat casually on the raft, deep within our own emotions and thoughts. There was no conversation. From time to time one of the men would suddenly lose his balance and topple into the water, demonstrating the distance from our mental to physical selves.

I began to consider the reaction of the families of my shipmates when word arrived notifying them that their loved one was dead. During the war the next of kin lived with the hope never to see the Western Union messenger bearing that yellow brown envelope with the ticker-taped message inside that began with the dreaded words, "I deeply regret to inform you . . ."

The war was over and we had escaped that tragic experience. All our families waited for now was word of when their loved one was coming home. Responding to that knock on the door would be a happy event, the moment before receiving good news. They'd greet the messenger with a smile and a friendly word, absent any apprehension. Then they would open that envelope and there would be those first three words. Every mother, every wife would be overcome with terror before finishing the message.

I was unable to change the direction of my thoughts. Events that had taken place not twenty-four hours earlier would now affect so many good people so profoundly. Instantaneously with the receipt of that simple, dreadful, succinct but clearly worded telegram, the future would be unalterably changed for the worse. Some of them would never again be the person they were the moment before opening the telegram. Children would never know their fathers, mothers and wives would never again hold their loved one in their arms. Although unknown to me while I was on the raft, my wife Dorothy and my parents received such telegrams about me.

Early that first afternoon on the raft the rain returned for a time but dwindled away. The mist lingered and our visibility did not improve. I was immersed in my thoughts with my head in my hands, staring into the water. From time to time I glanced up and scanned the ocean hoping to see some sign of any other survivor but there was never anything but the waves and foam.

Suddenly, I caught a movement in the water. My head jerked up and excitement ripped through my body like a jolt. I was instantly alert and focused on what had caught my eye. "Shark!" I shouted, pulling myself erect, jerking my feet out of the water. "*Shark!*" I pointed.

The men shouted and scrambled atop the rim, all eyes fixed on the fin. The men in the water hurriedly pulled themselves out. We all sat with our legs curled up, every part of our body on the narrow balsa wood.

I could see the telltale triangular fin protruding above the surface of the water, moving slowly and gracefully directly at me. For a moment I caught sight of the shark's entire body. It was ten feet in length, slightly longer than the raft itself. I spotted one eye and I was certain the creature was looking directly at me. Words are not adequate to describe the terror I experienced at that moment.

I looked closer as the shark drew toward us. Half a dozen other fins, all of them moving at us, surrounded him. *Was this our ending, then?* I thought. *Have we survived all this only to succumb to a fate worse even than that suffered by our shipmates?*

EIGHT

Sharks

Aboard any ship at sea the greatest fears are fire and capsizing. Adrift, on the remnant of a raft, our greatest fear was sharks. For all the horror I had visualized of shipmates dying below deck when the ship had turned over during the raging storm, even that fate seemed mild compared to imagining myself in the jaws of a shark.

Every eye was fixed on the fins as the sharks drew closer. Now they were no longer heading directly at us but rather were moving slowly about in no pattern that I could make out. They appeared to be performing some elaborate dance. As a body they were drifting along with us. I knew nothing of the behavior of sharks and did not know what to make of this. Were they waiting for some signal or movement on our part to attack? *Maybe they haven't seen us*, I let myself think. Then, the first one separated from the others and seemed to come straight at me.

My heart was in my throat as I waited for the moment of the attack.

I could see an eye again and was certain it was fixed on me. Yet, in another sense, the eye seemed unnatural to me. It was like those glass eyes you find in museums, tucked into the skulls of stuffed or re-created animals. It was lifeless, opaque, oddly blank as if it didn't see at all, utterly alien from anything I had ever seen before. Because of that, it was very frightening.

We were absolutely defenseless. My mind forced me to imagine what such a monster did to its prey. I could visualize it attacking my legs, pulling me from the raft, dragging me screaming under water, only to be attacked again by its powerful jaws, torn apart by razor sharp teeth, perhaps midsectioned, tossed about like a rent rag doll.

Did sharks actually eat humans or would it only maul me? Would death come immediately? Would I lose consciousness after the first attack? Or would I suffer from agonizing pain as it repeatedly struck until I ultimately succumbed?

Somewhere I had read or heard that sharks do not attack unless they are threatened or agitated. I remembered learning they would strike from hunger or if their territory was threatened in some way. We weren't agitating them while we were sitting motionless on the rim of the raft. Were they hungry? Was there any way I could tell?

The worst of it was that no matter what the cause, if a shark wanted, it could attack and there was nothing I could do about it. We were utterly within its power if it chose to act. We were in their waters, in their environment. Any shark was more powerful than any one of us, its large jaws partially open, exposing sharp edged, serrated teeth. They, not us, were in control.

The only possible weapons we possessed were a flashlight, a pair of pliers, a pocket knife, a piece of string, and a few bits of wood flooring. There was no doubt about whether the sharks would win a battle if it came to that. Watching the one shark swimming closer at its leisurely pace, seeing the fins of the others just behind it, I was paralyzed, waiting, watching to see what fate had in store for us.

The ocean was still quite violent when the shark made its first pass, coming very close to the side where I was. If my legs had still been in the water it came near enough to have brushed them. I could easily have extended my hand and grabbed its dorsal fin.

With the shark closing on the raft I could see McQueen's eyes widen in alarm. Without saying a word, McQueen grabbed at his knife. Either Hicks and Harrison, who both were sitting near him, saw what he was about to do and said in a sub-dued but harsh voice, "Damn it, Niles, don't you dare!" Both men grabbed McQueen's arm and held him back from stabbing at the shark. We all responded, trying to calm him down before he doomed us. We kept a close eye on him now. Here I'd been wondering what would happen if I touched the creature. I could only imagine the horrible consequences, the feeding frenzy that would have ensued if McQueen had tried to stab it.

I realized I was holding my breath. I eased the air from my lungs as the shark passed the end of the raft and continued on. If you can say anything about sharks, they are indeed very sleek and incredibly graceful. Their gracefulness can be tranquilizing and mesmerize you into a false sense of security in their pres-ence. As quietly as they glide by they can just as easily, and unexpectedly, turn and attack with great fury. I kept my eyes glued on the creature as it swam off some distance, its fin finally all that I could see.

Other fins were still there, not far away. The sharks were swimming slowly among themselves as if they had no interest in us but drifting along with the direction of the raft. It was a vast ocean. Why were they here if not for us?

I looked back to the first shark and watched it make a lazy turn, then head again toward us. All I could imagine was that it had made its survey and was now coming in for the attack. No one on the raft was speaking, no one was breathing. It came at us just as it had the first time. Again it made a close pass and continued swimming on, ever so slowly.

There was no way to know what was going on in its mind. I thought for an instant that it might only react from instinct, like a viper snake. If that were true there was no way to predict how it would respond, no matter how still we remained. At any moment, compelled by primitive drives we could not comprehend, it could turn on us.

I had heard that sharks had a very keen sense of smell but extremely poor vision. It seemed to me that the combination would likely create in its behavior a sense of caution. Smell is imprecise by its nature. If sight can't be trusted, then a shark might very well approach prey with uncertainty, awaiting events or the actions of the other sharks.

Was the one shark trying to get a better look at this massive object overhead? Was it scouting to see if our raft was a source of food, something it could eat? Was our raft too large for it? Or was it not hungry at the moment? Was it holding us within reach, waiting on its appetite? Clearly it was interested in us but at this moment it was not acting aggressively.

The lead shark passed a third time, as leisurely as before. Once beyond the raft it made its lazy turn, then came back again, and then again. The passing minutes were agony but there was nothing any of us could do but wait and remain utterly motionless.

From the first moment we knew there were sharks near us not a word had been spoken other than to Niles. Nor had there been the slightest movement on the raft. We sat as if hypnotized by the moving fins and the terror struck by the sight of the lead shark's massive jaws. Those rows of teeth, those triangular-shaped teeth, those razor sharp, serrated teeth! I could almost feel the teeth sinking into my soft flesh. The gripping jaws would drive those teeth to their full depth. Then the muscular body, that ten foot mass of muscle, shaking its prey, tearing away the flesh, bite by bite. With every pass it stalked us.

A half-hour later the shark slowly moved on, followed by the others. They did not disappear all at once or move off with an obvious purpose. They continued as they were, swimming gracefully among themselves, then slowly drifting away after the lead shark lost interest in us. I felt as if they had been summoned by some form of communication and were gone now amid the powerful waves. How far they went or when they would return, we had no way of knowing. From that time on, we stayed within the confines of the raft and kept our eyes carefully on watch for the menacing fins.

When we began to speak again we relived the experience, finally coming to a group decision that the sharks did not have good vision and that the raft with the suspended rope netting presented an object too large for a shark to attack. Hanging from the raft or dangling our legs on the outside of the ring, we decided, was too risky.

The experience had shown us that this was their ocean, not ours. We were the intruders, not they.

The seas had quieted to the point where the cresting waves no longer overturned the raft. If we had been tossed off when the sharks were beside us I had no doubt what would have happened. It would have been a feeding frenzy and many, even most of us, would not have survived.

Since the morning of the previous day we had survived two of nature's greatest threats to man: a typhoon and the dreaded shark. What would be next? I wondered.

My mind returned to the three men on the flying bridge. I had been certain they were in our vicinity, drifting with us. Maybe that was why the sharks had not been hungry. Maybe the sharks had already found Blaser, Stauffer, and Engler. Maybe that was why we couldn't find them? Because . . .

Stop! I couldn't allow myself to think it but I couldn't help *but* think it. It was a question to which mercifully I would never learn the answer.

I often think back to those sharks. The situation was so bizarre. We were completely defenseless and entirely without control over what was happening. I had heard conflicting stories about sharks attacking people. We knew little about them in 1945. I had been told that sharks do not target people because we are not a natural prey for them. They might attack by mistake, which explains why humans are often bit. But it is an instinctive reaction when it does happen. That's why sharks kill so few people. But I had also heard that sharks do attack people.

I wasn't sure what to believe. What I experienced gave me no answers. Why had we been spared? We had absolutely nothing in our favor. We lacked speed and strength, we weren't camouflaged, and we had no weapons for self-defense. Yet the sharks had passed us by. There was no answer, but the memories, the fears, are still with me and always will be.

As our first day on the life raft progressed, the sea grew less ominous although the mist lingered and obscured our distance vision. We scanned the nearby water continuously and saw no sign of the sharks' return. The raft was small for nine men so none of us was far from the other, yet we said little. We were together but in a much more profound and significant way we were apart.

Late in the afternoon Hicks suddenly straightened up and pointed. "Is that a ship over there?" he said.

We all looked. Each of us could see, just faintly through the mist, an outline of a small ship, dropping in and out of sight, riding the crests and troughs of the still strong seas. I watched closely and determined it was heading directly at us. *So this is it,* I thought. *As easy as this after all we've been through.*

Everyone agreed it was traveling directly toward us. There was no question we would be spotted in just a few minutes and would soon be onboard a ship. We'd be warm and dry, eating hot food, drinking all the fresh water we could hold. Sleep, though, was the one luxury I most wanted. I needed rest for my battered body and surcease from my thoughts and memories.

We could hardly contain our excitement. We had overcome all odds in surviving a major typhoon and had cheated the sharks.

I soon could see the ship quite clearly as she made her steady way toward us. She plowed into the rough seas, creating a great sheet of white water as she nosed into each wave. None of us had expected salvation so soon. We had resigned ourselves to at least one more night aboard the raft, thinking that no rescue was likely before the next day. But here was our rescue ship, as natural as that. We slapped each other on the back, shook hands of congratulations for our survival, grinned until our faces hurt, shouted for all to hear the first thing we planned to do once onboard that wonderful ship. We had cheated death and soon would be back with our loved ones.

With my flashlight I tried signaling the ship as she continued heading straight at us. I aimed the light directly at her. I sent the distress signal of three dots, three dashes, three dots. I made the ship to be a quarter mile away. Although I doubted the vessel could see my light because it was still daylight and there was a heavy mist, it still made sense to try.

We watched the ship draw closer and closer, striking each wave with a massive surge of white water over her bow. Then suddenly she stopped dead. Why had she stopped, we asked. What's wrong? For several minutes she bobbed in the waves, stationary.

Several of the men began to wave at the ship. We all shouted. "Here! We're over here!" Then, the ship was under way again. But as she moved she also turned away from us at a right angle. "No! Here! We're here!"

We watched in disbelief as the vessel continued on her new course until she vanished from sight into the mist. We were dumbfounded, speechless! We watched, hoping she would return, that she would resume her course, that someone on-board had seen us. We imagined the ship was only delayed a few minutes before rescuing us. But no rescue happened. We never saw the ship again. I cannot describe our sense of loss, the despair that overcame each of us.

I later learned that the ship had been the tug ATA-188, which had been sent to assist USS *Shellbark* (AN-67). The tug had spotted bodies in the water and turned to pick them up. They found George Wade, the farm boy from West Virginia, who I'd seen so lonely, staring off across the water. Wade was found alive, afloat in a life jacket. Not far away they spotted Bob Hobart, that wonderful young man with the boyish face and wide grin. I had last seen him working the radio, desperately seeking contact with other ships. How he could have escaped the radio shack and made his way through and then out the bridge I could not imagine. He and John Foster, who had also been in the radio shack, had tied their life jackets together so the storm would not separate them. The pair must have emerged from the bridge just moments after we had all jumped in the ocean to grab the life raft before it drifted out of sight. Both men were dead when pulled from the water. Because Wade, also in a life jacket, had survived but Hobart and Foster did not, I suspected sharks. I never did learn their fate.

Considering it later, I concluded that others on the bridge must have found their way out as well. They had just been slower than those of us who managed to get on the raft. When the other men had stood on the side of the ship they must have found the life raft gone, vanished. Had they called out for us? The howling wind would have swallowed any human cry. Finally, forced to abandon the sinking ship, the men had probably leaped into the raging tempest, commending themselves to the mercy of the wind and waves with nothing but their life jackets to save them.

Although the tug had encountered one survivor and the bodies of two others, I feel it failed to conduct even a cursory search of the area. Logically, if three were found, there were almost certain to be more. Also, the captain should have alerted other nearby ships, which could have moved into the area and assisted in the search. The weather was good enough despite the rough ocean to launch planes to search for more survivors. Instead, the tug pulled three from the sea and then resumed her original course.

At the time, however, I knew none of this. Aboard the raft we talked about nothing but the ship and speculated endlessly. We were convinced she would return to pick us up. We rationalized our predicament by convincing ourselves in the way desperate men will that the ship had gone for help. She would come back, if not this day because nightfall was fast approaching, then surely the next. At the least there would be a flurry of activity as the navy began searching in earnest for survivors.

As night approached problems began to manifest themselves. It had been a day and a half since any of us had slept or had anything to eat or drink. We were utterly exhausted. We were hungry, but more importantly we were thirsty. I noticed both Perry and Ash sneak sips of sea water. Once again I cautioned them about the dangers of doing so. All of us were tempted and I almost envied them because they had, at least temporarily, eased their thirst. It took great discipline for the rest of us to avoid the temptation.

As night fell we each knew there would be no relief from the thirst and hunger for the next twelve hours of darkness, nor was there any chance of rescue. Balanced as we were on the rim of the raft there was also no opportunity to sleep although all of us had become very sleepy. Ahead of us stretched a long, dark night. It descended over us in moments. I found the dark oppressive. It left each of us in greater isolation. My mind turned again to the shark encounter earlier that day. I had visions of sharks swimming right alongside of me, waiting for the slightest opportunity to strike. It was so dark I could not possibly have seen a shark or even its fin.

I was not the only one filled with such fears. We all sat with our legs in the water inside the ring of the raft, convinced the rope netting offered us a measure of protection. Yet the slightest movement in the water near us or the motion of the netting dangling in the water caused immediate panic. We could see nothing but we were certain sharks were bumping against our legs. I waited in terror, wondering when a shark would make its final attack, pulling me off into the night and tearing me apart before I was devoured.

From time to time one of the other men would speak in a subdued voice, "I think there's one next to me. Don't move." We would hold our breath, make no motion of any kind, and wait. As the night passed we became more accustomed to the feel of the water and our raft's netting so we became better at discerning them for what they were.

On a few occasions during that second long night we heard and even spotted planes above us. We watched their running lights in the sky. I repeatedly signaled the distress code with my waning flashlight. One plane actually flew quite low and near us. I was certain the flashlight could attract its attention but by this time the batteries were nearly dead and the light had become very faint. The plane passed on with no acknowledgment. I finally discarded the flashlight in disgust.

Perry and Ash had the least clothing of any of us. As the night wore on they lowered themselves into the water inside the ring of the raft. The sea was moderately warm and shielded them from the chilly night air. If we had anything in our favor it was the relative benevolence of the temperature of both the water and air. The air was neither cool nor warm but it did turn cooler during the night. The sea itself was not especially warm but it was not uncomfortably chilly, so Perry and Ash had decided it was better for them in the water.

Because we could have no meaningful hope until dawn the night lasted interminably. Our fatigue, sleepiness, hunger, and thirst, most of all our thirst, tended to heighten our impatience and anxiety. The night stretched on and on with no end in sight. It was agony for each of us.

None of us slept, although from time to time each of us nodded off. Because we were sitting on a bit of wood only nine inches wide whoever did fall asleep often toppled into the water. Waking up, he would then scramble quickly back aboard.

In the hours before first light Perry and Ash began to talk about food and water. They could not seem to help themselves. Although we asked them not too, they persisted. It was, I believed, no coincidence that these were the two I had seen drinking sea water. Food, and most of all water, were the two subjects we were all desperate to keep out of our thoughts. Our throats had become parched and our need for water never left us. The last thing we wanted to hear was talk about thirst or water.

There was nothing to do but wait for the darkness to pass. Perry and Ash talked on about food and water no matter how much we tried to discourage them. I wondered for the thousandth time if the night would ever end.

NINE

Dawn of Day Three

Dawn slowly dispelled the black of night. With the coming of morning we began searching the water and sky for any sign of rescue. The fierce winds had turned into gentle breezes. Even the once powerful waves were dramatically reduced in force and size. While there were still whitecaps, the crests were no longer lifted off as they had been previously. The sun attempted to break through clouds that were thinner than before, although they still largely blanketed the sky. A morning haze that promised to dissipate replaced the mist. The best news was that there were no sharks in sight.

With the sea and the winds improved we no longer had any trouble maintaining our balance on top the rim of the raft. Most of us sat with our feet dangling in the water inside. Some men were hanging in the sea, their arms wrapped around the rim and their bodies pendulously suspended within the confines of the raft.

Our raft was a tiny pinpoint in that vast ocean and we were intimidated. In every direction we looked all we could see was uninterrupted sky and ocean. Did anyone even know we existed? We didn't know. Was anyone searching for us? We were confident they must be, but we had no way of knowing for certain. Did the ship that had turned away from us the day before see anything to report? We hoped so.

The irony of our predicament did not escape me. The war was over and our time of danger had supposedly passed. The casualties should have ceased. Yet, here we were, casualties of this incomprehensible disaster. I could not help but think back to the many problems we had suffered during our ship's ten-month tour of active duty. And what of that steady stream of thirteens? Did they mean anything? Had they been an omen? It certainly crossed my mind.

The thirteens, considered alone, were at least thought provoking. What had the odds been for such strings to occur repeatedly? Taken with the frequent problems the ship had experienced, the final incident with the anchors in Buckner Bay made the entire picture jump into place. The incidents, the number thirteen, seemed to possess a meaning, to have been a warning we had chosen to ignore. It was an upsetting picture that formed in my mind and I was not alone in these thoughts. Despite our mishaps and the concerns over the thirteens, the morale on the raft that morning was good.

None of us had sleep for any period of consequence the previous two nights so we were exhausted. Besides the physical abuse we had sustained during the typhoon we all suffered from anxiety and tension. It is difficult to describe the debilitating effects. For all our optimism we still knew our situation was perilous. If nothing else, the sharks had served to remind us just how tenuously we clung to life. If they returned and targeted us we would vanish within moments.

Still, we believed we had cause for optimism. We had had no expectations of rescue the day before yet it had nearly occurred. Today was the day we were certain we would be found. Hobart, who had been manning the radio, had surely been able to put out our position and plans, and one of the other ships must have made note of them. We were also certain that when we failed to reach Unten Ko and had not been heard from or seen since, someone would conclude that we were missing. Surely, in such a violent storm, other ships had capsized as well. With that known, a combined sea and air search would already be under way and we could reasonably expect to be spotted and picked up shortly.

The return of daylight and the moderating weather no doubt added to our optimism. We had every reason to expect rescue. The resources available to the U.S. Navy on Okinawa were immense. We were drifting perhaps only sixteen to twenty miles from the island. The war was over so all the ships and planes, all the highly trained and experienced personnel, had nothing else to do. These assets had been marshaled on Okinawa in enormous quantities for the final assault on Japan, which had been mercifully cut short by the use of the atomic bomb. With demobilization, equipment might simply be abandoned. In the case of the men, they would be sent home when their number came up. It is unlikely that ever in the history of mankind had so many resources been available to conduct an air or sea search and rescue. We all knew this and it was just one more reason why we continuously scanned the sky and sea for planes and ships.

Later that morning we observed Portuguese men-of-war drifting near the raft. Although normally brightly colored, these were pale, nearly transparent, with a floating sac from which tentacles extended suspended beneath in the water. The tentacles could deliver an excruciatingly painful and poisonous sting that could bring on infection. More and more of the jellyfish arrived. Before long as many as a hundred surrounded us. When they drifted close we pushed water in their direction, attempting to force them off. Only one of the men was stung and it wasn't serious. Eventually the breeze or sea current floated them away.

Talking more this morning, our conversation covered many topics. Our missing shipmates were on our minds. Could they have made it? We questioned one another about where we had last seen each man. We speculated as to whether or not it would have been possible to escape the ship from where each shipmate was at the time of the capsizing. We had already talked a great deal about Blaser, Stauffer, and Engler. We were certain they had to be in the same general area of the ocean as we were. With the calmer seas we could now survey a much larger area than the day before but neither they nor any other evidence of our ship could be seen. There was absolutely no evidence of the sinking within our sight and we could not understand why there was not even flotsam from our ship.

We speculated about what happens to a ship as it plunges into the depths of the ocean. Surely a ship constructed of wood broke up during its descent. If so, where was the wood? Where were all the other loose, buoyant materials within the ship, much of which surely had escaped through the open doorways or hatches? This was, and remained, a mystery to us. As far as we could tell the only evidence of the sinking was our small, damaged raft, the flying bridge decking, the orange float, and us—the nine souls on the raft.

We also speculated about the many other ships that had left Okinawa when we did. Some must have successfully made it to Unten Ko. Wouldn't they be making their way back to Buckner Bay by this time? We were certain we had capsized somewhere just off the northeast tip of the island. The wind and seas were moving us to the northwest, placing us directly in their return path. That being the case we should be seeing ships coming toward us from the west. We looked constantly in that direction but nothing came into view.

Our physical discomfort grew with each passing hour. We had leaped into the raging water from the side of our stricken ship one and a half days before. Our lower extremities had been submerged in salt water ever since, and our upper bodies had been immersed for long periods of time as well. Sea water had been splashed onto our faces almost constantly so that our faces were in a continual state of wetting and drying.

With the calm weather and bright sun, our upper bodies, and in particular our faces, were now encrusted with salt residue. Our dry lips were noticeably swollen and cracked. Our parched mouths had no moisture and we could not wet our lips with saliva. Our exposure to the sea elements and our dehydrated condition became more painful.

As engineering officer aboard ship, I had spent considerable time in the engine rooms below deck, going in and out of them several times a day. The ladder into them was very steep. When I climbed up the ladder I routinely struck my shin against the next rung, halfway between my knee and ankle. The constant contact created a permanent bruise that until now had caused me no real harm. My legs had been submerged in salt water almost continuously since the sinking and a very painful infection had set in where the bruise was. Sea water ulcers had also grown on my lower extremities and were now painful with every move. We were all suffering more and more.

Even though the ocean surface was smooth, there was a constant lapping of water against the edge of the raft. It served as a recurring reminder of our desire to sip refreshment from the ocean. Our compulsion to satisfy the demands of our parched mouth for moisture to soothe our dry and cracking lips was never ending.

It wasn't just water. Our stomachs ached from hunger. We were tortured with thoughts of succulent, tantalizing food to satisfy our pains. In the absence of any sign of a search there was no release from the cravings that filled our every thought. When I was growing up in Aurora, Illinois, I worked as a carrier for the local newspaper. Every Saturday we turned in our collections from the previous week and at that time received our pay. Mine was two dollars plus five cents for each dollar of collections I had made. My normal collections were about sixteen dollars. I would turn the two dollars over to my mother to help with the household expenses and the remainder was mine to spend as I wished.

During the summer months I would walk to the local ice cream parlor after receiving my pay. I would buy my favorite drink, a Black Cow, made by placing a scoop of vanilla ice cream in a large glass of root beer. On a hot summer's day, there was no other drink that was as satisfying. With the thirst and hunger I was experiencing while drifting in the raft, my thoughts turned increasingly to a desire for a Black Cow from the ice cream parlor in Aurora. Visions of that frosty glass with the tangy effervescent bubbling of the root beer as the cold ice cream settled to the bottom of the dark glass invaded my mind and refused to leave. The desire to have just one of those drinks was overpowering. No matter what I tried to think about to relieve my mind, the thought of a Black Cow returned. At one point I vowed that if I survived this ordeal I would never pass an ice cream parlor without going in and having one.

About midmorning a large plane flew over us, at a relatively low altitude, but a bit off to the side. Several of us waved our arms hoping to draw the attention of someone aboard, but it kept on going with no signs it had seen us. This had been the closest passing of a plane yet, but it was gone quickly and we weren't optimistic that we had been seen. The raft was gray and there was very little contrast between it and the color of the water. We were also the smallest of specks in the largest ocean on earth. We had hoped to be spotted but really didn't expect it and we weren't. The plane never veered in its course as it flew away toward the horizon.

Very quickly we reverted to our pervading oppression and despair. I struggled desperately every moment to erase the constant thoughts of that thirst-quenching and hunger-satisfying Black Cow by replacing it with other recent memories of events aboard ship. I forced myself to think of our arrival at Saipan earlier that month. There had been the usual chores of taking on provisions and fuel and picking up what we all eagerly waited for, our forwarded mail. Blaser had gone to the command ship to check in and to receive additional orders for the Okinawa leg of the passage. It had been there that he was given a directive with the news that four shipmates possessed enough points to qualify them for immediate discharge.

There had been much discussion about the new point system as we had crossed the Pacific. We had learned that four lucky men were eligible. However, the directive ordered that only two of the four leave the ship at that time and return to the United States for discharge as soon as transportation was available. The two men were put ashore on Saipan. Although happy for them, we were also envious. Our turn would come, we knew. We sailed on to Okinawa without replacements.

The other two qualified for discharge were Shockley and Frye. They were considered essential to the safe operation of the ship and no replacements were available at Saipan. They had to remain with the ship until qualified replacements were found. They had stayed aboard a ship that proved to be doomed. Both of them were with the ship when it capsized. And neither was with us.

There had been another event that was unforeseen and it bore startling results. Our original steward's mate had several bouts with venereal disease and had been replaced. He left the ill-fated ship and a replacement came aboard in Hawaii. The replacement went down with the ship. The man who had been a disgrace to his uniform was alive because of it, while the good sailors who had done their duty were dead. It's true, "Life is not fair."

As the day grew warmer we languished in the sun—thirsty, hungry, numb from lack of sleep. From time to time, one of us fell face first into the water, startling the rest of us. Sitting on the rim of the raft, I would occasionally open my eyes and gaze into the water. One such time I noticed a school of fish swimming just below us. They were meandering in a lazy pattern, drifting with the raft. I mentioned it and others began to watch them. "Can we catch one?" someone asked. A good question.

They were relatively small fish, perhaps a foot or so in length. They came so close to us we could nearly touch them with our dangling feet.

"What about that string?" another said. We had some thirty inches of string but no fishhook or anything we could turn into one. Maybe if we dangled it in the water one of the fish might bite on it. We talked about this and convinced ourselves to give it a try. Our thinking was that we could clearly see the fish so when one bit the string we would see it and quickly jerk the fish up. We thought the fish would keep biting on the string long enough for us to grab it. We vainly tried to maneuver the string around in front of the fish trying to entice one to bite, but we couldn't generate any interest. After a half-hour the fish slowly swam away.

I continued to look for fish, hoping they would return and give us another chance to catch them. What I saw instead was six or seven hammerhead sharks, perhaps five feet in length. I had never seen a hammerhead before and knew nothing about them. Strange-looking creatures, they had wide sideways-extended heads. They were swimming at some depth, perhaps ten to fifteen feet down. None of us grew alarmed at their presence because the thought never crossed our minds that they might be dangerous.

I had noticed earlier in the afternoon that Perry was beginning to put his head in the water as if to cool off, but I thought I detected something else. Sometimes it looked as if he might be drinking the sea water. I watched him and I saw him do this several times. Then a little later I saw him cup his hands and bring the water to his mouth and swallow.

We had talked about the possibility of merely wetting our mouths with sea water. But we agreed that we had to spit it out and avoid swallowing it. It was obvious Perry was drinking the water. It wasn't long before I saw Ash doing the same thing. Having cautioned against this earlier, I again reminded them of Rickenbacker's story and of the consequences of drinking the salty water. The warning seemed to register and they stopped.

We sat in a stupor, our eyes closed or fixed into the water or off toward the distant horizon. In the midafternoon Hicks scanned the ocean and drew my attention to an object coming into view from the west. I looked and it appeared to be a ship, maybe more than one. Everyone brightened at once. Rescue! Salvation! Could this be the search party?

It was difficult to see across the glassy water and I had to squint. We starred intently and finally made out four ships coming plainly into view and heading in our general direction. They were small ships. At first we couldn't make out the class. As they drew closer and closer we all agreed that from the look of their silhouettes they were YMS minesweepers.

Now we were certain they were a search party looking for us. Our spirits soared. With the bright, clear sunlight and extended visibility, we were positive we would be found. It was only a matter of time.

We never took our eyes from the four ships. As they drew closer to us we realized they appeared to be sailing in line, one behind the other. They were going in a direction that would take them some distance to our south. They were moving west to east. We speculated they were returning from Unten Ko, headed for Buckner Bay. En route they were searching for us. That only made sense. We were known to have left Okinawa with all the other ships. Even if Hobart had failed to contact another ship that would have relayed our plans, we had not reached Unten Ko and had been out of radio contact for nearly three days. We were known to have been lost in the typhoon and survivors would be in this approximate area of the ocean. They had to be searching for us, and for the survivors of any other ship that foundered.

But the closer they came the more it became obvious to us that they would pass a considerable distance south. They were not spread out in a search formation, nor were they zigzagging in a pattern to cover the greatest possible surface of the sea. It looked to us as if they were sailing in line, moving inexorably, and blindly, back to Buckner Bay. Before they were gone we tried to figure out some method of attracting their attention. All we could come up with was to remove our T-shirts and wave them over our heads. There simply was nothing else we could do.

Although the ships were clearly not in a search pattern we persuaded ourselves that they were covering the area to our south and would soon make a turn and head more directly toward us. We continued to wave our T-shirts with no reaction from any of the ships. We watched, dejectedly, as they sailed on out of sight. We waited and watched intently for their reappearance from the east. As the hours passed, one by one, we gave up hope and accepted that the ships had not been searching for us. They were simply sailing back to Buckner Bay. We returned to the gloom and solitude of our inner thoughts.

Several of us made the mistake of not putting our T-shirts back on. The warm sun shown directly on our bare backs and I'm certain more moisture was taken from me than would have been otherwise. Fortunately, my good suntan from our passage across the Pacific kept me from burning on that part of my body, but I surely lost water.

The passing of the four YMSs and their failure to return, along with the lack of evidence of an air search, proved an answer to the hopeful question of the existence of a coordinated search for us. We concluded there was no search.

If those ships were on a search, they would have made a return sweep by now. If there was an air search we would have seen some indication of it by now. If the weather and heavy clouds had been a deterrent the previous day, today offered ideal visibility with calm seas. There would be no better condition in which to conduct a search. The answer was all too obvious. No one was looking for us.

As the afternoon passed, little or nothing of note took place. There were no problems with waves or wind because the weather remained clear and comfortably warm. We saw no shark fins, nor did we spot any planes or additional ships. It was dull. Our brains were active due to our fears and heightened anxiety, but our thoughts were blunted by our deteriorating physical and mental state. There was nothing in view to break the monotony, nothing except the ocean and sky, nothing to take our thoughts from our fear and distress. We sat motionless, starring blankly ahead, feeling nothing, increasingly isolated one from another.

A few puffy cumulus clouds high in the sky appeared late in the afternoon. Later a darker area formed in them and brought hope of a squall or light shower. We watched intently as one did indeed develop into a shower some distance from us. We could see the falling rain, but it was out of reach to us. We talked briefly of trying to paddle the raft to it but gave up on the idea. It was just too far away from us. Even if we had been able to reach the location it would almost certainly have been over by then. We watched as the cool, fresh water fell from the sky. Within ten minutes it had stopped.

The pain in my leg grew worse throughout the day as the saltwater ulcers exacerbated. The one that had formed just below my knee was quite large. There were three more on my ankle. Others had formed on my right leg and there were some on my buttocks as well. Although all were discomforting, only the one on my left leg was infected.

I lifted my leg out of the water and rested it atop the raft. I placed my foot on the rim and took a good look at the festering sore. A reddened area extended an inch or two around it. It felt better in the open air than it had submerged in the sea water. I took a good look at the other ulcers. They were just sores about the size of a five-cent coin and didn't appear or feel to be infected.

Sitting with one leg lifted up on the rim was uncomfortable, however, and I couldn't keep it like this indefinitely. There just wasn't enough room. After a half-hour I changed position and put my leg back in the water. The sore had dried so when I placed it in the salty water the pain was excruciating. Luckily the pain lapsed somewhat after a few minutes.

The pain in my leg presented me with a dilemma. I knew it would be better to keep my leg out of the water but on the other hand I couldn't sit for long periods with my leg and foot resting on the rim of the raft. Several times I lifted it out. Each time I put my leg back into the water the pain was agonizing. There was no permanent solution and I had no way of knowing if these short periods of drying were making any positive difference. Worse, the moving aggravated the ulcers on my buttocks. In the end I gave up and left my legs in the water.

After so many disappointments, and given my deteriorating physical condition, it became increasingly difficult to attain, or even maintain, a positive attitude. I began to feel defeated. Night was fast approaching and I knew we all dreaded the coming of darkness with its interminable length. We could see nothing in the dark, not even one another, and there could be no hope of rescue. We lost all track of time at night. We were trapped in it. Night meant utter loneliness. Night meant despair born in solitude.

With the approach of nightfall I began to worry about both Perry and Ash. Would they again start to drink the sea water in the darkness of the night? With their obvious weakness to resist, would the temptation be too great? Would others succumb to the temptation? Would I? The blackness of the night and the frustration brought on by the hopelessness could create the desire to take that first sip.

As night fell we spoke among ourselves to alleviate our loneliness. With our words we gradually convinced one another that we were surely drifting toward land. The earlier disheartening events made our minds susceptible to any positive suggestion, anything that offered hope that we could embrace, any thought that offered salvation. Our state of high suggestibility was greatly enhanced by the darkness. So convinced did we become that we paddled furiously, heading, we believed, for land.

As we paddled we were convinced land was nearby and that we were nearing it. We began to hear voices. We could smell the cooking fires. The aroma of the food, the sounds of voices, all lent credence to our belief that we were close to land. We paddled all the harder toward the sounds and smells. From time to time we stopped, listened closely for the voices to be certain we were on course, then resumed our furious paddling. For all I knew we could have been paddling in circles. The voices continued and the smell of smoke, of frying bacon, became more pronounced. We shouted over and over, so everyone would know we were out here, so that if we were swept away someone would look for us.

We were convinced that the people we heard talking would hear us in turn and respond. We shouted and shouted for as long as our voices held out. But there was no response. Why didn't they answer us? We waited and waited for the light of day to come so we would see them and ask them face to face why they had ignored us.

I cannot explain the phenomenon. For occasional short periods, we would return to lucidity and someone would say, "Why are we doing this? We're not close to anything. There's no one around. There's no cooking!"

The logic and persuasiveness of the words would pull us back to reality for a time. But inevitably we returned to our delusional thinking. Within our fantasy was hope and salvation. We shared certain smells and sounds but each of us also had our own private delusions, carefully constructed to remove us from the reality of our plight and to give us a hope we otherwise did not feel.

I didn't understand why we reacted in concert to the voices and to smelling cooking fires. We all acted as if we were hearing and smelling the same thing, at the same time. All of us shouted, "Can you hear us?" or "We're here! Over here!" in a vain attempt to draw someone's attention.

Finally, exhausted from our paddling, unable to reconcile the sounds we heard with the unwillingness of the people uttering them to respond to our cries for help, we were reduced to sitting in a stupor, wrapped within the cocoon of our own fantasy state. We waited and hoped as the suffocating blackness of another endless night kept us blanketed in our tiny world, cut off from one another. The night was without limits and reduced us to insignificance.

TEN

Dawn of Day Four

On the previous morning the slowly rising sun had eased its light through the thin cloud layer. The coming of day had brought hope, a renewed belief that at last, somehow, someone would rescue us from this nightmare. This was all we desired through the long horrible night.

The morning of our fourth day, 19 September, was different. The clouds were black and the air was hazy with visibility only a few miles or so. Daylight should have come with an uplifting of our spirits. The warming sun that we had anticipated was not to be seen and an early morning chill lingered on.

Despair was clearly visible on every haggard face, just as I'm certain it was on mine. No one spoke about what we were not seeing. No words were needed. We all knew what had taken place during the night and it exposed us to be even more fragile and desperate than we had imagined.

I say all of us were aware, but I noticed that Perry and Ash were acting a little different than the rest of us. Somehow they didn't seem to be concerned about the events of the night and were unconcerned about what awaited us during the coming of day.

We said almost nothing about what had happened and there was little conversation as the morning hours slowly progressed. Most of us on the rim of the raft sat with our head in our hands and our elbows on our knees, eyes closed, trying to sleep. Even though the seas were calm, someone losing balance and tumbling face first into the water would interrupt our dozing every few moments. There was a steady sound of splashing as the morning wore on.

The need for water had become a constant nagging to take that one sip of sea water. Resisting the urge became more difficult as the clouds began to break and the day warmed. But both hunger and our need for sleep were also becoming major factors in our struggle to maintain sanity.

Several times during the morning we all saw Perry and Ash drink from the ocean. I admonished them, as did the others, even appealing to them, with no effect. No matter how forcefully we begged, we were completely ignored. From their actions it seemed they no longer heard us.

In despair I realized that Casleton, one of my engine room gang, and such a fine young man, was also losing his willpower to resist the water around us. He too began taking an occasional sip of the salty sea. I cautioned him about the dangers, as did the others. He would acknowledge us and stop for a time, but then I'd see him cup his hands and furtively drink once again. I was more convinced than ever that, just as Eddie Rickenbacker had warned, once you succumbed to the temptation and took a small sip of sea water, the desire to drink even more became overwhelming and the will to resist was forever lost.

We couldn't comprehend the reality of our situation but every indication was that no one was searching for us. Our lives were reduced to happenstance. Luck was our only hope, and how long could we hold out? Perry was fading, Ash was not far behind, and now Casleton was on the verge of following in the same path.

Who would next surrender to the tempting, refreshing water that surrounded us? This was what those of us who resisted that temptation so far talked about. Our enemy surrounded us. Time was what we needed if someone was to stumble on us by accident. We began questioning the useful life of our life jackets and of the raft itself. We noted that several of the jackets were now missing. Some of the men had carelessly let theirs drift away so we had just five life jackets for the nine of us.

By that same perverted logic that overtook so many of our decisions in such desperate straits, we decided that only four of them were still in good condition, although we held onto all five. Because no one was wearing a jacket we no longer knew which belonged to whom and decided to hang onto them as a group.

The raft was another matter. With relatively calm seas we were now able to see how far the raft was floating above the water line. Just two inches was visible. We were certain the rim of the raft was floating much lower in the water than it had been previously. It was losing its buoyancy. How much longer would it stay afloat was the only question. Would *we* succumb first? Or would the raft upon which we depended for life?

Our conclusion was that the raft did have a finite life, one that would come to an end in the not too distant future. This realization caused us to be even more protective of the life jackets, especially as there were not enough for all of us. We kept the jackets out of the water and no longer let them float as before. We wore them or carried them on our laps.

As the morning wore on, little or nothing of note took place. There were no problems with the waves or wind. The skies were generally clearing with a few low-hanging clouds on the horizon. We were comfortably warm and we saw no shark fins. We also didn't spot any planes or ships. I can only describe the day as dull. Our brains were active due to our fears and heightened anxiety, but our thoughts were blunted by our deteriorating physical and mental state.

There was nothing in view to break the monotony, nothing except the ocean and sky, nothing to take our thoughts from our fears. We sat motionless, staring blankly ahead as a pervasive numbness crept through us. Feeling nothing, our isolation from one another increased.

On occasion we would become alert enough to search the horizon or sky, looking for, and wishing for, something to give us courage to hang on. Finely, Harrison, said, "Hey, I think that's an island over there!" He pointed. "Look over there! I've been watching it. At first I thought it was a low-hanging cloud, but I think it's an island."

When the rest of us looked, it wasn't clear if there was an island or not. The low-hanging clouds had an irregular shape that resembled the tops of mountains. Or were they really mountains? We stared at them for some time before someone more positively said, "They have to be mountains. Look, the clouds are disappearing and the tops of the mountains are still there."

Most of us agreed we could see that *something* was sticking above the horizon. Others could not initially, but as time passed we all agreed there was an island nearby. Perhaps it was Okinawa itself, but there were many small islands in the area into which we were drifting. It made no difference. It was land. It was escape. The war was over so it did not matter if the Japanese occupied the island so long as it was solid, dry land. Our spirits, including Perry's and Ash's, soared.

We all had experience at sea and each of us knew how deceptive distances across water could be. Yet we persuaded ourselves that the island was within our reach. Once we agreed land was not too distant we began paddling toward it, using our arms and hands as well as the strips of wood flooring that we still possessed.

We didn't have to float helplessly, waiting for someone to find us. Our fate was in our hands. We could make it! Lacking paddles, however, we found the raft very difficult to maneuver. Our optimism inspired us but it was the lack of food, sleep, and especially of water, as well as the expectation of none in the foreseeable future, that caused us to paddle ever harder to reach the island.

We allowed no negative utterances as we toiled, trying to paddle our way to safety. One of the men slipped inside the perimeter of the raft and kicked his feet. It was like he was clinging to the side of a swimming pool and learning to swim. The rest of us paddled as fast as we could with our hands.

Working furiously, we talked constantly, one on top of the other. "I think we're closer!" one would say. Then another, "No, we're not, we're moving away!" Our spirits rose with each optimistic comment and fell when someone said something negative.

The effort to reach the island took all of our energy and attention, but it consumed a good portion of the day. By midafternoon we decided that it was hope, rather than reality, that had caused us to believe we had actually drawn closer to land. Still, we let nothing interfere with our efforts. Above everything else we feared being swept away from this island. If that happened, we would be losing our last possibility to reach land and would drift off into the vast Pacific, far beyond any hope of rescue.

By now our mouths were completely dry. Our lips were so cracked they ached. There was no escaping our thirst, especially because we were surrounded by water. It was becoming more and more difficult to resist that temptation of one little sip. Thankfully Perry and Ash were able to help in the paddling effort. However, on occasion I could see them, and Casleton, drinking from the ocean.

There was no organization in what we did, there were no rest periods. Maybe there should have been, but no one appreciated how exhausting this was going to become. As time passed, no one spoke any longer about reaching the island. Each of us could see for himself the unpleasant reality.

For more than seventy hours, almost three full days and nights, we had been without food, water, or sleep. We had in that time fought an unbelievable battle with the elements to survive. We had now spent most of this day exhausting ourselves even more. Our strength had been below par to begin with and this fruitless effort only broke us down further. In the end, our efforts served only to aggravate our problems and diminished our ability to withstand the as yet unknown ordeal that still lay ahead.

With sinking spirits we eventually accepted the truth. The current was causing us to drift out to sea and away from the island. The effort dissipated our stamina and left us emotionally destitute. We had failed to reach the island! That realization was bitter.

Finally, exhausted, depressed, one by one we stopped and sat on the rim sucking air into our lungs, licking our parched lips, squinting at the still distant island. All our effort had been for nothing.

The journey from euphoria was by this time quite rapid. Each hope had become higher. Therefore, each successive down became lower. Depression settled over us. It was midafternoon and not one of us wanted to spend another night on that raft. We were even more exhausted and much thirstier than we had been at dawn. Our condition was only going to grow more desperate the longer we remained at sea. None of us had any idea how long we could survive without food and, most of all, water.

Our hopes of rescue were greatly diminished. We were quite discouraged. If we were to be saved I believe each of us was convinced we would have to do the saving. Finally, one man spoke, expressing the thought on all our minds. "Maybe we should swim for it," he said. There were murmurs of agreement. No one wanted to surrender themselves to the sea. No one wanted to give up the hope that the island had come to represent. Each one of us wanted to end our ordeal by swimming to the island. If we were unable to move the raft to it, surely someone could manage to swim the distance. After all, we still had some life jackets.

Our encounter with the sharks two days earlier, as well as the hammerheads we had seen the day before, should have blunted our willingness to swim ashore, but we had seen no sharks today. We were exhausted and feeling desperate. We pushed thoughts of sharks aside. We were so convinced we could make the swim that we didn't consider the danger sharks might represent.

As the only officer on the raft, it was my decision to make. Should we make the attempt to reach the island by swimming for it? It was an easy choice. The only alternative was not acceptable to any of us. In fact, I doubt it was within my power to have prevented any attempt any man made to swim for shore.

"Okay," I said, "I think we should try for it, but only two of us. They can send help once they make it." There was the nod of heads in agreement. I also reasoned, but I didn't say it, that if they failed in the attempt the remaining seven would still have a chance of rescue.

Who to send? Everyone wanted to be selected. Obviously, Perry, Ash, and Casleton were not good candidates for the swim. There would be great risk. If they failed, even forgetting the sharks, they would be swept to sea held afloat only by their life jacket, a spot in that vastness that would have been very, very difficult for anyone on a ship to see and impossible for someone on an airplane.

I was persuaded that the chances for strong swimmers reaching the island were good, although not without risk. I put the odds at better than fifty-fifty, which seemed good considering our circumstances.

I didn't know how far away the island was. I didn't know how much energy anyone had left after our grueling effort paddling. Desire, I knew, needed to be a major factor when I made the selection. The more strongly the swimmers were determined to make it, the more likely they would succeed. Physical condition would also play a role. Who was in the best shape?

I looked around the raft. All eyes were fixed on mine. I saw in each man the desire to be chosen. Luckily, I did know a little about everyone's swimming ability. On many occasions we had anchored in some bay and members of the crew would dive off the ship and swim. I knew the best swimmers among us. As for physical condition, I would just have to make an educated guess.

I did make one decision I didn't utter. I eliminated the married men with children. There were three, so that left only three others from which to choose. "I know you all want to do it," I said. "I understand. Okay then, Talley and Hetzer, you two go ahead." The pair grinned at being selected. Words of approval and encouragement came immediately from the rest.

Hetzer was not talkative and, if anything, a bit somber in his manner. His first duty in the navy was on YMS-472 when he had joined us in New York. In contrast, Talley was quite upbeat, talkative, and always smiling. He had been with the original crew and was known as the ship's clown. Although a little chubby, I knew he was a strong swimmer. I thought both men were in good shape.

No one objected to my selection. We all spoke about how the effort would be a complete success. "Don't forget us when you get to shore," more than one said with a laugh. But there was no doubting the seriousness of the words. No one wanted to spend another night on the raft. We picked out what we thought were the best of the four good life jackets. Once they were secured, the men were ready to go. It didn't take long. With good-byes all around and a final reminder to send help as soon as they could, they set out with enthusiasm, eager to reach the shore.

Having discarded his other clothing that first night as we fought the storm, Talley only wore a pair of undershorts and his life jacket. Hetzer was wearing full-length navy blue jeans and he opted to not remove them.

Although I had mentally estimated the odds, all of us at that moment were positive they would make it. They had jackets to keep them afloat so they could rest from time to time if necessary. With a steady pace and a determined effort they should be able to make it.

We had tried repeatedly to estimate the distance to the island but our estimates varied widely, from as little as one mile to as much as six. Neither of these distances should be a problem for Talley or Hetzer. Because we sat just a couple feet above the water's surface, we knew from that elevation that the horizon is not far away. Therefore, a relatively distant shoreline would not be visible. How clearly we could see the land meant nothing because clarity at sea is not determined by distance but by the amount of moisture in the air. We simply had nothing on which to base our estimates. What was true was that the more we talked, the closer the island became. Wishful thinking and desperation were playing an important part in our judgment. The mind in times of extreme anxiety has a tendency to ignore reality.

Each of us watched the pair as they swam away from the raft, heading for the shore, picturing ourselves in their place. They swam strongly and I was satisfied with my decision. They hadn't been gone so much as a minute and were no more than twenty or thirty yards from the raft, however, when I heard a horrible scream. Hetzer turned about at once and swam toward us as if possessed. When we realized who had screamed, we shouted, "Talley! Talley! Are you all right? Talley!" There was no answer. We yelled, then waited for a reply. Someone thought he heard a weak reply. We yelled again. Nothing. There was splashing in the water where Talley had been but no sound from that spot reached us.

Within moments a hysterical Hetzer reached the raft. In his desire to get out of the water he was flailing about with his arms. It was difficult for us to grab him and help him aboard. He was screaming the whole time, as desperate and frightened as I've ever seen anyone in my life.

Once he was on the rim Hetzer pointed frantically back to the way he had come and said, again and again, "Sharks! Sharks!" He was frantic, his eyes darting madly one direction then another, searching for shark fins.

"Look!" one of the men said with despair. We could now see a blood stain in the water. We all knew that blood drove sharks into a feeding frenzy. We began paddling as fast as we could away from the blood to put as much distance as possible between it and us. Our paddling was no more effective than it had been in trying to reach the island. After a time we could no longer see the bloody patch so we stopped.

After Hetzer quieted down he told us what had happened. "We were swimming together," he said in a rattled voice. "We were not more than a couple of feet apart. Then Talley said to me, 'Did I just kick you?' 'No,' I told him, not knowing what he meant. Then a shark grabbed him, maybe more than one, I don't know, I couldn't see. Anyway, they attacked him and dragged him under the water. He tried to scream but they got him under the water." Hetzer was sobbing at the memory. One or two words of consolation were spoken. No one else said anything. What more was there to say?

Two days ago, when we had seen the sharks for the first time, we had discussed their possible temperament. We had found no answers to our speculation. Our unanswered questions had given us hope, hope and the expectation that sharks were not as treacherous as we had feared.

Now we had our answers; now we knew the truth. There was no escaping reality. Sharks were all around us. They were vicious, savage killers who could pull us down and devour us at the slightest opportunity.

I sank into despair. I had picked Talley and now he was dead. The attack had been sudden and quick. The first strike had taken him under the water before he could make a sound. He had come again to the surface. Whether the shark still had him or was about to make his second strike we couldn't know, but he was taken under the water a second time. It was then that he had made that weak cry for help, if that was what we actually had heard.

I imagined the vise-like jaws and the long, piercing teeth, tearing through flesh, penetrating to the bone. Then the coordinated, wild thrashing, shaking, and whipping of the head and massive body of the shark as it ripped Talley's flesh to sheds while he was still alive. I could only pray he had been in a state of shock and numb to what was happening to him.

Earlier, I had hypothesized what a shark attack was like. Now we knew. An attack had played out in front of us, just a few yards from our eyes. What happened after the thrashing I just couldn't imagine. It was too painful to contemplate.

Was this to be our fate then? Were our lives spared during the capsizing and sinking of the ship only to come to this? Were the sharks lurking just out of sight, waiting to mount their next attack? Did they wait until they were hungry? Were we their personal food locker?

There were no answers but now anything seemed possible. I knew, we all knew, there was no worse fate than what had befallen Talley. Was this the fate each one of us would inevitably face?.

We had speculated endlessly about what had befallen our other shipmates. Did they escape the ship before it went down? We had hoped against all hope that they were floating out there in their life jackets. There had always been that distant prospect that they had miraculously survived, although we knew now that was a remote possibility. We knew without any doubt that we had lost at least one member of our ship's crew. What chance, I thought, did anyone have floating out there in a life jacket? Could any of them still be alive?

Within my despair and black thoughts, I wondered what could have caused the attack. The sharks had been with us, swimming alongside of us a couple of days ago. They never once made any attempt to attack. Of the two, Talley was wearing the least clothing. Perhaps the sharks had been attracted to his swimming by his bare light skin and white shorts. Maybe their curiosity had been aroused and they had drawn closer to explore. Busy swimming, Talley would have been unaware that the sharks were just beneath him. Maybe he had accidentally kicked one of them, thus provoking an attack. I thought this scenario was more likely than his having been mistaken for food. We were always available if food was what the sharks were after.

Hetzer remained visibly shaken. His eyes continued to dart about as he searched for sharks. None of us saw any. I don't know what we would have done if we had. We knew they were there. Why couldn't we see a dorsal fin? Without realizing it, we had unconsciously made the decision that if there were no fins visible, there were no sharks. What a mistake that had been! Now we knew that fins or no fins we were in shark-infested waters and that sharks were killers willing to attack. We were confined to the limits of the ring of the raft. No one was going to attempt to swim ashore. We were like cattle abandoned in a corral.

We were now reduced to our only option: waiting for someone to spot us. Earlier that morning we had seriously thought this was the day we would see something, some sign of an organized search—airplanes or ships combing the nearby area. We expected to spot a plane or ship in the distance, some visible sign people were looking for us. We had seen nothing.

We were demoralized. We couldn't reach the island and there was absolutely no indication of a search. The only planes we had spotted were very high, too far above us to see us. The only ships we had seen the day before did not appear to be on a search. This was why we had tried the swim for shore. That attempt had ended in disaster and the loss of a shipmate.

Sitting on the side of the raft contemplating all that had passed, feeling dejected and demoralized, I noticed that Perry, sitting on the side of the raft opposite me, was looking at me in a peculiar way. He appeared to be staring intently at me. Then he began behaving strangely. He entered the water within the ring of the raft. Floating there, looking at each of us in turn with a slightly puzzled expression, he wore an innocent expression. After some time he said in a very calm but serious voice, "I'm thirsty, I need something to drink."

"Yeah," I said, "but we don't have anything. All the provisions are gone."

Paddling over to me, he stared steadily at me. He then said, "I know you have some Coke hidden on the raft. I want some."

"Hal, I don't have anything," I answered. "You know that. There's no place on the raft to hide anything. Why would we do that? What are you talking about?"

Perry became more dogmatic as he spoke repeatedly of the Coke I had concealed on the raft. He became quite argumentative. "I know you've got Coke and food too! I'm going to report you to the captain if you don't give me any!" He moved within the raft with purpose now, systematically looking under the rim for the secret cache of supplies. All of us were confused by his behavior. When he got to me he grabbed my leg where I had an inflamed saltwater ulcer and started acting as if he thought it was a bottle of Coke. He gripped it very hard and tried to pull it to him.

"Damn it, Hal. Stop it! Now stop it! That's my leg! I don't have any Coke or anything else to drink. Just stop it! And stop talking about drink or food, or anything like that! We're all in the same predicament. There's nothing! We've just got to tough it out. We're all in the same boat."

It did no good. Perry continued in the same vein. Only now it was not just about food and water. He began talking about beer. Perry insisted that there were cases of beer and Coke hidden somewhere on the raft. He repeatedly accused me of hiding them, saying I wasn't sharing with the rest. He continued threatening to report me to the captain.

I tried to reason with him, as did the others. We explained that there was no place on the raft to hide anything. I couldn't understand what in the world he was thinking. It was so obvious that nothing could be hidden on the small, thin canvas-wrapped ring on which we all sat.

What he was saying was beyond logic, but I gave no consideration to delusions setting in. I had never been exposed to such a mental phenomenon before and it simply did not occur to me. Perry just seemed to be outrageous and dogmatic. I thought I could reason with him. But no matter what I said Perry talked constantly about hidden beer and Coke. I was baffled as I tried repeatedly to explain how illogical it was to think that a case of anything could be hidden on our small raft.

While this was going on, Ash, who had also been drinking sea water earlier, remained silent. A glassy look appeared in his eyes and he also began acting strangely. He looked right at me, but wasn't focused on me at all. "I have to go and see how the horses are doing," he announced. "They're out in the pasture feeding and I need to go check and see if they need water."

This made absolutely no sense. I didn't know what he was talking about or what was going on. Ash, I knew, had never lived on a farm and knew nothing about horses. I could not have been more perplexed. We all argued with him, persuading him to stay on the raft.

Perry remained on his mission within the ring of the raft searching for the hidden supplies, talking constantly about his thirst and the need for Coke, water, and beer. We argued repeatedly with Perry and told him to be quiet. "Damn it, Hal, shut up! Stop talking about food or water! You're just making it hard on all of us. Just stop." But it did no good. Nothing changed.

Ash's behavior, although not as extreme as Perry's up to this point, rapidly deteriorated. He was soon acting in a similar irrational way. He began to ramble on about his thirst, his words often incomprehensible. His eyes had a distant, not of this world, look. From time to time, without preamble, he'd say, "I'll go see if the horses need water." Luckily we were able to convince him to remain with us.

Perry appeared to be fading fast. Ash was not far behind. Now Casleton was drinking sea water more frequently. How long could any of these men survive?

I knew we were all fatigued from the paddling to reach the island and the mental anguish we suffered over the tragic loss of Talley. The approaching day's end and the anticipation of no relief before nightfall was obviously having horrible effects on all of us.

Late in the afternoon, when Perry wasn't pleading for water or a doctor or babbling about the Coke I had hidden somewhere on the raft, a distant look was fixed on his face. His eyes would stare far off, not fixed on anything. He still threatened to report me to the captain for not sharing, but less vehemently. I understood by now that he was suffering from delusions but had no idea what, if anything, I could do about it. Others had tried to reason with him as I had, but to no avail. None of us fully appreciated the seriousness of his condition. Even if we had, there was nothing to be done.

Perry decided to give up on me. If I refused to share the Coke I had hidden away on the raft he would find his own. Now he was convinced that our ship, the minesweeper YMS-472, was immediately below us, resting in shallow water within easy reach. The ocean floor was in fact more than one mile beneath us. We had drifted many miles from our ship's final resting place. Still, Perry was certain that all he had to do was to dive under water to find the Coke. And that's what he decided to do.

He would slide from the rim of the raft and swim underwater, attempting to dive down to the ship. He did this repeatedly. Each time some of us would jump into the water after him. We would pull him back to the rim and persuade him to climb back on it. A few minutes later he'd dive again, trying to reach the ship. When he wasn't in the water he would threaten once more to report me to the captain.

"When I get to the ship," he'd say, "I'm going to get beer from the galley." Then he'd slide off the raft and try to swim down to the galley in the ship. It was difficult to get him back on the raft and we had to struggle forcibly with him each time. Once on the rim he would remain calm only a short time, then the delusion would begin again.

There was no doubt all of us were nearing our limits, both physically and mentally. Some were deteriorating faster than others, although most of us were still sufficiently lucid to grasp reality, at least most of the time. Still, the events and physical exertion of the past four days, along with the lack of water, food, and sleep, were getting to us.

Thirst was a constant and continuing problem. The demand to satisfy it was unrelenting. Hunger, on the other hand, manifested itself in a gut-wrenching pain that came and went with time, sometimes lasting for what seemed like hours. I could feel the growling coming on as I looked around the raft for something, anything, to eat. I spotted a leather belt on Hicks, and it looked tempting. I looked down at my own belt and decided to try it. I pulled it from my pants and began chewing. It had been soaked in salt water so I hesitated for a minute for fear of the salt residue. Yet I continued to chew, ultimately succeeding in tearing off and swallowing a few bites. I gave up on it before devouring it completely. The pain, however, as well as the day, wore on.

Toward dusk, Ash's behavior began to deteriorate even further. It was if Perry's delusions were infectious. Ash now also insisted that YMS-472 was directly beneath us. He said, "You know the ship is just below us, in shallow water, I can go down and get some orange juice from the engine room." He said he could dive for her and get to the engine room where the engine room crew kept a supply of juice. All he wanted was his share, no more.

Nothing we said to him made the slightest difference. Ash remained certain that the ship was just below us. He was adamant about the orange juice in the engine room and just as adamant about going down for some.

Several times before dark Ash slid into the water and tried to go below to get orange juice from the ship. "Grab him!" one of the men called out. Again the rest of us dived into the ocean to rescue him. When we pulled Ash from the water he would respond, as would any person in a normal state of mind. His meandering into and out of rationality was not as severe, nor as frequent or as long lasting, as Perry's. However, when Ash was experiencing the delusion he was just as convinced as Perry that the ship was immediately below us.

As twilight faded into night, Perry, Ash, and now Casleton, were jabbering away, reinforcing their conviction that our ship was beneath us. Everything they desired—water, juice, food—lay within their grasp. From time to time, with no predictable pattern, one, two, or all three would slide into the water in an attempt to reach the ship. Given their state, I am certain that if we had not pulled them back they would have eventually been lost and drowned. But the effort it took to retrieve them extracted a heavy toll on us.

The other five of us luckily remained almost normal in our thinking. Hicks, McQueen, Harrison, and myself would nod off from time to time. Hetzer, still excited from his near encounter with the shark, continued to nervously scan the ocean surface for the telltale shark fins. Although exhausted, it was not possible to sleep in any real sense because we were so precariously perched on the narrow rim of our raft. The instant we fell into a deep sleep we toppled into the water. As a consequence, we never slept long enough to overcome our exhaustion.

Often when we recovered from falling into the water, we would observe Perry, Ash, or Casleton thrashing about or diving and looking for the ship below us. Over and over we pulled them onto the rim, using up what precious physical resources remained to us.

When complete darkness enveloped us, I was plunged into a profound despair. Although the hours of daylight and darkness were approximately equal, the nights seemed so much longer than the days. With daylight there was always hope of rescue. In darkness there was none. Night served to isolate us from one another further and further.

In the darkness, once again, our imagination and longings filled the void for our senses. We heard voices quite distinctly. We could smell frying bacon. Again we shouted, and again there was no response. Despite our experience the night before and that morning, we were all certain that we were drifting toward an island. We believed that at any moment we would be stepping off the raft onto dry land and salvation.

I cannot explain our obsession with this fantasy. I can only think our increasingly debilitated condition, our numbed senses, and our desperate need compelled us to create hope. We moved between irrationality and lucidity with disheartening ease. Our inability to determine what was real from apparition continued. During the times we spent in our more-or-less-lucid states, we still suffered from residual delusions. During our less-than-lucid states, our thinking was equivalent to those we knew who were not fully rational. We fully shared in their fantasy of sounds and voices.

Although we could snap out of our delusions, we soon reentered fantasy worlds. Our movement back and forth, between rationality and fantasy, occurred in unison. I don't recall there ever being a time when I was lucid and everyone else was delusional, nor do I recall coming to and noting that everyone else was clear-headed, waiting for me to return to normal with them. Although the rest of us had our periods of rationality, Perry, Ash, and Casleton remained longer, and more profoundly, within the grasp of their fantasies.

Throughout that long night Harrison, Hicks, Hetzer, McQueen, and I repeatedly found Perry, Ash, or Casleton in the water, searching for our ship. We struggled with less and less enthusiasm to pull them out. In time we began to tolerate their conduct in silence. Finally we left them alone as they thrashed and dived about.

Time moved with excruciating slowness. We struck no island. In the dark, in our isolation and struggle to remain sane, our despair reached new depths. After what seemed a lifetime, when I felt I could bear the night and hopelessness no longer, I detected the faintest of smudges in the distance. Night had passed.

ELEVEN

Dawn of Day Five

At first light, in the distance an island was visible. We stared at it, afraid to allow ourselves to feel any hope. "Look, isn't that smoke drifting up into the sky?" Harrison asked. For several slow minutes we watched and discussed whether or not we were seeing smoke or just a small cloud hanging below the mountain peaks in the distance. We strained our eyes as we blinked repeatedly to clear the dry film over our eyes. Other clouds were visible higher in the sky, but this one was much lower. Finally, as much to satisfy our desire as for any tangible reason, we decided it was smoke. And smoke meant people. No voices in the dark this time! No imagined smell of sizzling bacon! This was real, or as close to reality as our circumstances allowed us.

We discussed the island, especially how far it was from us. We agreed in the end that this would be our last hope. Our desperation dictated that we had to reach the island no matter what it took. We had no plan and did not discuss the decision logically. Jointly made and almost as one, most of us placed our open palms into the water and began to paddle. We gave no thought as to how much of our flagging energy this would cost or what price we would ultimately pay. Once again, we believed we had no alternative.

Not everyone understood what we were doing or joined in the effort. Perry was nearly in a catatonic state, sitting passively, without movement. From time to time, in as normal a voice as any of us still possessed, he would ask for water. No one would answer.

Casleton had apparently heard me say, "Paddle!" and decided I had said, "Pedal." He sat astride the rim of the raft and furiously churned his feet in the water as if he were pedaling a bicycle. It was no help at all, in fact it likely worked against the common effort, but our repeated shouts to get him to use all that effort to help paddle were in vain.

Like Perry, Ash neither paddled nor pedaled. Instead, he placed his hand on the surface of the water and worked intently at smoothing the small wavelets our movement created, like a child passing his hand over the ripples in sand.

None of us really understood how far these three had deteriorated so we were angry with them for not helping. From time to time one of us would shout, "*Paddle* damn it! Don't pedal! We need you to *paddle!*" But our exhortations did no good. Nothing I said, or anyone said, caused Casleton to stop pedaling his bike. "Stop clowning around, George," I'd say. "We've got to reach that island. Can't you see it! We need you to paddle to get there! Help us! There's an island over there.

Now, damn it, start paddling or we won't make it!" It made no difference.

And it was no different for Ash or Perry. Ash continued smoothing the ripples in the water while Perry sat as passive and immobile as the Sphinx, except when he uttered his occasional request for water.

Part of me was convinced that the raft was riding much lower in the water than it had been the last time that we had tried to move it this way although this was not true. We were in far worse physical condition, though, and only five of us were actually making any effort. Any apprehension I felt over the declining state of the raft, however, or doubts about our ability to reach land, were suppressed, masked completely by my determination to reach land. We were certain this was our final chance to survive.

McQueen and others cut the hanging rope netting away because we were convinced it made the raft more difficult to move even though up to this point we had always believed it gave us a measure of protection from sharks. We talked briefly about the resistance caused by our legs, which were also in the water, but there was no place else to place them.

For approximately the next six hours we paddled without letup. At the height of our exhaustion, when our parched mouths were raw from sucking air, we were compelled to accept that the island was no closer. As with yesterday's efforts, today's land was now more distant from us than when we had begun. We were moving parallel to the island. The current was drawing us quickly past, then ultimately away from it. When we had started paddling, the island had been directly in front of us. As the hours passed and we were swept by, it now appeared to our right.

Exhausted beyond description, one by one we stopped paddling. We had no choice but to admit to ourselves that we could not move the raft to land, no matter how hard we tried.

We had all been at our lowest when daylight had finally come. The island, and the hope of rescue, had lifted us emotionally. We had kept our spirits at a high pitch during the hours we paddled, encouraging one another, not permitting any negative comments. We had been fixated on just one thought: Get to that island! Plunged again into despair, we resigned ourselves to defeat. I'm sure each one of us faced again the certainty of our inevitable death. During our long days adrift our fleeting highs had always been followed by lows, each one worse than the previous one. This was the worst ever!

We knew this was our last hope. We *had* to do something! When at last we could speak, someone, I no longer recall whom, said that one of us had to swim to the island. The only other alternative was to continue drifting until all of us were like Perry, Ash, and Casleton. We knew what that would mean. We had seen no sharks during the day, but knew from experience the dreadful outcome when swimming with sharks. They were almost certain to be out there. It would not have mattered, I believe. We had no choice! There was no talk of Talley's fate, no mention even of the potential danger from sharks. I am convinced that even if we had seen sharks that day we would have persuaded ourselves that someone had to make the attempt, and at least one of us would still have been willing.

Hicks, Hetzer, Harrison, McQueen, and myself were still capable of lucid thought. We discussed our situation among ourselves. As before, physical well being was a consideration. We had deteriorated physically since Talley had died making his attempt. This time I made no decision, nor did the group, because McQueen announced that he was going to make the attempt no matter what we decided. He was an obstinate, uncompromising man. I am certain that if we had decided someone else should make the effort, McQueen would have gone regardless.

I knew he was a strong swimmer with as good a chance as any of us. Even if I had recalled at the time that he was a loner who tended to look out for only himself, it would not have mattered. He was a shipmate. I trusted him. After selecting what we considered to be the best of the jackets, one that Harrison had been protecting diligently from becoming waterlogged, McQueen strapped it on.

As he slipped into the water, we pleaded, "Do you think you can make it! Niles, be sure you get to the island no matter what it takes!" Every word we uttered was tinged with desperation. We knew the time left to us was no longer measured in days. We watched McQueen swim away from us and shouted after him, "Send someone back before sunset, Niles! For God's sake send help! We won't make it through another night!"

"I will," he assured us. "I'll tell them you're here."

In our state of mind, clinging to tatters of hope, we all thought it certain that McQueen would make it to the island. Long after he was no longer visible we stared in the direction he had vanished. In time, we imagined we saw him reach the island and rise to his feet on the shore. As with our night voices and smells this was not possible. After he swam beyond our sight, it was impossible to see him reach the island, yet we convinced ourselves that we had—such was the urgency of our desperation.

After we saw McQueen reach land, we continued staring toward the distant island. Now we imagined we could see people and boats entering the water, coming toward us. Help, we told one another, was on its way.

Throughout the fading afternoon we watched for the arrival of the boats. We vacillated between having no hope at all to absolute certainty that the boats were approaching. Our imagination and our hope played terrible tricks on us. As the hours passed our increasingly brief moments of certainty that rescue was coming were matched by even longer times during which we knew there was no rescue, leaving us feeling isolated and abandoned. Finally, as if releasing its dying breath, our hope vanished utterly. McQueen had not reached the island. We had seen no people. There were no boats. We would not be saved.

What lay before us was another bitter night, one that each of us dreaded. Our agony reached a level we had not previously endured. Even we four most-lucid men suffered spells of confused thinking. We slipped in and out of delusional thinking, accepting the fantasies of Perry, Ash, and Casleton.

Their condition became extremely serious. Perry knew I was hiding beer and Coke on the raft just as he knew that our ship was lying beneath us in shallow water. He was certain that all we had to do was swim beneath the raft and we would find the ship with all the provisions we could ever want. By this time no one made the slightest serious attempt to persuade him otherwise.

Each one of us no longer cared about the state or activities of anyone else. We had become convinced that McQueen had failed to reach the island. That meant he too had been attacked by a shark, or drowned, or swept out to sea to die drifting in that life jacket. Not one of us expressed any sympathy for his plight. We had become incapable of expressions of emotion for others, although our instinct to protect and help one another remained. We slipped in and out of our delusions with regularity and increasing frequency.

When we returned to lucidity we would look around at the others and often realized that either Perry, Ash, or Casleton was absent. Sometimes more than one was missing from the raft for short periods. They would swim out of sight, then, as they returned we would instinctively drag them onboard.

Although Perry was in the worst shape of all, Casleton was rapidly deteriorating. He told us that there was a ship tender nearby. In Buckner Bay, as elsewhere, we had drawn our stores from such a ship. Casleton was no longer the good-looking ladies' man. He was haggard, as were we all, and completely consumed by his fantasy world. He swam far from the raft and remained away for longer periods of time, although he always returned. Harrison, Hetzer, Hicks, and I were often in such a state that we eagerly awaited for Casleton's return, expecting him to bring supplies that he had obtained for us from the ship tender.

Delusional states continued. More and more frequently, and for longer and longer periods, we believed the fantasies of Perry, Ash, and Casleton. When our thinking was close to normal we understood how absurd these thoughts were, but this did not prevent us from lapsing back into the comforting world of delusions. We elaborated upon them, shaping them to reflect our own special obsessions and needs.

Perry was also altering his delusions. He was relatively quiet for some time, as if he were deep in thought. Then, late that afternoon, in a normal voice, as if he were making casual conversation, he said, "We can catch a cruising taxi. It'll take us anywhere we want to go. The driver might even have something with him for us to drink."

We were confused by what he was saying, especially as it came from right field. We wondered among ourselves what he could be talking about. Our efforts to dissuade Perry, however, were half-hearted as each of us longed for the cruising taxi. Maybe one of those cruising cabs *would* come near us and we could flag it down.

The more Perry talked about catching a cab and taking it to shore and all that such a thing meant, the more elaborate his scheme became. He explained that the floor of the Pacific Ocean contained a sprawling network of huge, connecting tubes. He was convinced, as Ash soon was, that there existed a fleet of taxicabs cruising about in these tubes. All we had to do was hail a cab and it would drive us to an island. Our mental condition was such that all of us, at one time or another, were equally persuaded. We had become so susceptible, so subject to suggestion, that the fantasies of one easily transferred to the rest.

Hicks, Hetzer, Harrison, and I would occasionally return to some semblance of rationality and would recognize how outlandish our thinking had been, how weird our thoughts had become. Although we did not speak of it, I am certain each of us worried that there would come a time when we would no longer return to normal thought, when we would remain permanently within our fantasy world. In one sense we knew it would be the ending of ourselves, so we resisted delusional thinking. In another sense our dream world possessed a powerful appeal. If we gave ourselves over to it we would be released from our grim reality and the looming certainty of our fate.

Knowing our thoughts were delusional for long periods did nothing to prevent our slipping back into them. We engaged in fresh fantasies, fervently embellishing them in elaborate detail. The greater we enhanced the delusion, the more convinced we became that our hallucinations were reality.

In discussing Perry's tube scheme, we became perplexed over how the cabs picked up fares. In time, we decided that the tubes had manholes on the surface of the ocean. This had the effect of making the fantasy even more tangible to us. We could enter the manhole. From there we could make our way to the vast underwater network of tubes. We speculated as to how such a system would work and what a manhole on the surface would look like. Our speculations added strength to the idea. Within a short time it seemed entirely plausible. We feverishly paddled helter-skelter searching for a manhole, cursing that they were so far apart and difficult to spot.

Our fantasies were something we needed deep within us. Even when lucid, we put aside logic, disregarding any thoughts or comments that would suggest a new idea was not possible. We ignored any reality that came between us and any imperfect plan we concocted. We had to maintain hope! We manufactured new ideas to support the old, devising elaborate explanations to prop them up. We said and presumed anything to avoid a negative thought that might cast doubt on one of our vital fantasies. When hope faded as one fantasy failed to produce relief, another was invented or expanded to fill the void. Our fantasies were an unbroken string, each leading to the next without interruption. The process of creating or elaborating on each idea filled the span of time. In addition, the time between the fantasies within our delusional world and our ideas devised when we were normal was rapidly disappearing. In time, there would surely be no separation.

Our deviant thinking flourished because we were becoming increasingly desperate with the approach of night. This was for us the absolute worst time. With pending nightfall our susceptibility to wild thinking and comforting fantasies grew, as did our fear.

Just before dark we discovered a manhole adrift in the Pacific. Within the opening we saw a taxi driver, his head and shoulders quite visible. His arms were laying comfortably on the edge of the tube as he searched about for a fare. Although I can clearly picture the scene I have no recollection of the details of his features or appearance. If I heard his voice again—yes, he spoke to us—I would be unable to recognize it. But I remember him.

I talked to the taxi driver, spending some time inquiring about his service. I told him we wanted to go to Okinawa and Buckner Bay. I wasn't the only one able to hear the driver and received suggestions as to what to ask. The taxi driver expressed concern over how he would be paid. I assured him that the U.S. Navy was good for the fare. At this point I snapped out of my fantasy. But its appeal was so powerful that within moments I was once again seeing the taxi driver and resumed my discussion with him.

The taxi driver remained reticent about taking us so I offered him five hundred dollars for a ride to any island. He no longer had to take us to Okinawa. I assured him that I had money coming, and I would pay him myself. He wouldn't have to wait on the navy. While I was negotiating with the taxi driver, we didn't notice Perry swim away from the raft. During a period when some of us had regained our senses we realized that he was gone.

Perry never returned.

A fine young man, he had survived the Normandy invasion and been awarded the Purple Heart for wounds sustained during that bloody day so lethal to minesweeper crews working in close to the hostile beaches. He had been so quiet and unassuming, willing to do his part in any task, so very close to his mother. But I gave this no thought at the time. It seems peculiar, but while I could intellectually grasp the reality that young Perry had disappeared, I experienced absolutely no emotion about it at the time. Absolutely none.

I believe our reaction, or rather our lack of reaction, to Perry's loss was influenced in part because it occurred near dusk. We were consumed with our own powerful emotions and fears as night fell. We were of two conflicting minds over his loss. Part of us may have understood that he was gone, dead, or near death somewhere out there in the vast ocean. But our minds were muddled and our desperation concocted another fantasy. We no longer saw the taxi driver or thought about catching a cab. We believed Perry had taken the cab! Part of us hoped he would not forget us and would remember to send someone when he reached land. He was gone, true, but only because he had gone for help.

How is it possible to be so close to someone one minute and in the next know he's gone but have the realization create no emotional response? At best, I can conclude only that a part of me was seeking to shield myself from the loss. I recall our casual indifference to Perry's loss with revulsion. I know I was not thinking rationally but I can never forgive my lack of concern. I was alive, and as long as I lived, no matter how delusional the circumstances, I feel I should have been capable of genuine human compassion.

We were now six.

Perry had first devised the idea of the network of tubes on the ocean floor and the fleet of taxis. When he disappeared all talk about them stopped. The driver we had been talking to had taken Perry. In our state we could not conjure up another taxi driver.

Once again it was interminable night and we immediately descended into a profound depression at what lay ahead. Night stretched before us like a long black tunnel with no light at the end, no hope of seeing light until the long, endless hours passed.

Shrouded in darkness, Ash again spoke of our ship, still convinced that she lay in shallow waters immediately below us. It was as if this fantasy was necessary to fill the void created when we stopped engagement with the undersea tube delusion. As Ash asserted his belief the rest of us were drawn in. He slid into the black water again and again, diving in search of the ship. We pulled him back constantly, not merely to save him, but to see if he, in fact, had returned with something to drink. At the same time we engaged in the process of turning the idea into something that sounded perfectly reasonable. We elaborated upon our comforting fantasy.

In the black water below us we believed we could discern the green running light of our sunken vessel. From the light we judged the ship to be laying in less than twenty feet of water. After a few minutes I told the others that I had managed to create a voice tube down to the ship. It was the same kind of voice tube we had on the ship for the captain on the flying bridge to communicate with the bridge or engine room. I positioned the tube just as I would the real thing. Using the tube I was able to talk to the crew in the sunken ship.

We listened in the darkness, staring into the black water at the green light. Soon we heard the voices of our shipmates. We listened even more closely and could hear them playing cards, eating and drinking, and enjoying themselves in general. The man on the ship below, the one I was talking to, was Gildore, the gunner's mate who had always been such a discipline problem. According to Gildore, the crew survived within special rooms sealed from the water. Gildore said that our sister ship YMS-454 was also nearby on the ocean bed. The two crews had constructed a passageway connecting the ships, allowing them to freely visit back and forth by driving a Jeep. Some crew members were there at the moment, playing cards.

I gave Gildore our names and directed him to send up our back rations, especially Coke and beer. One of the men heard my request and convinced me to ask for food as well, if they were going to the trouble of sending us drinks. We relayed the actual number of days of back rations we were due and to which we were entitled.

I never liked Gildore because he had been the source of so many complaints and problems, so I've often wondered why he was the crew member my mind conjured up. I have no answer.

With my communication finished, we eagerly searched the water around us for our back rations from the ship. Waves lapping against the rim caused small white caps. The resulting foam had the slightest glimmer in the otherwise black water. The foam caught our eye and for several minutes we thought it was a sign of the supplies making their appearance. We clutched at the foam and slapped at the small waves, certain they were the drink and food we so desperately needed. As we grabbed repeatedly at the water, stirring it up in our frenzy and desperation, we reluctantly came to realize that our minds were manufacturing this fantasy. We forced ourselves to remain in a more logical state although we continued to believe our ship was just below. As with the tubes and taxis, it had been Perry who first argued that our ship was beneath us. Although the tube and taxi fantasy vanished with his loss, the ship below fantasy persisted.

Ash continued to press his argument that the ship was in easy reach. Casleton resumed his talk of the nearby ship tender. From time to time he swam out of sight to locate the ship, only to return empty-handed. His delusion never fully captured our imagination as the tubes or our sunken ship had. During his extended excursions we often kept careful watch for him. When he finally returned we shouted out to him the moment he was in sight, "Do you have something for us? Did you get it?"

In our fantasies we slid easily from one delusion to the other, sometimes talking about the ship below, another time about the ship tender, sometimes about both in the same breath.

Peculiarly, I was no longer tempted to drink sea water. I believe that I had so conditioned my mind against the danger that I had established an outright fear of it. My mind was focused entirely on water and food. From time to time I considered how we might get provisions from our ship below or from the nearby ship tender. I gave no thought of McQueen or of the possibility of rescue. I was utterly devoid of emotion and felt nothing for anyone, not even my loved ones back home.

Perhaps because so many hours were filled with our fantasies this night did not seem to pass as slowly as the previous ones. Very likely our condition had deteriorated to such an extent that even when we were lucid we were in varying degrees of stupor much of the night. Or perhaps we were now simply incapable of comprehending the passage of time in any normal fashion.

Far into the night a profound change occurred in the four most intelligible. The last of our fantasies slipped from our minds and each of us confronted his reality in his own way. The state of our minds was such that we were no longer able to concoct or maintain any aberrations. We lost track of the comings and goings of Ash and Casleton into the water around us. There was no hope in their excursions. It was as if our minds had surrendered. We sat in a daze on the rim of the raft, half asleep, half awake, only partially lucid. From time to time we toppled into the water. For a moment or two I would be rational but such moments quickly dissipated.

Our condition was probably much like that of Perry's after the third day. Although it seemed that while we were more cognizant for a longer period of time, once we started downhill we descended rapidly.

We did not encounter a nearby island during the night. Nor did we hear voices or smell cooking food. Just before daybreak, however, when our spirits were at their lowest ebb, we saw a dark object immediately ahead and convinced ourselves it was an island. We could hear the sounds of reveille and smell smoke from a fire, the cooking of bacon and eggs. There was music and the talk of people. But with first light, as before, there was nothing, nothing but the bitter, endless sea.

We were hollow by this time, no longer capable of reacting to anything other than from primeval instinct. We could no longer discern reality from fantasy. We existed only within our diminished selves. Our world was this tiny ring of balsa wood. If a great shark had pulled one of us from the sinking rim of the broken raft I am not certain any of the others would have so much as acknowledged it.

The night had been utterly debilitating. We met dawn but were no longer the men we had been at dusk. We were devoid of any human feeling. Any hope we had ever had was now gone.

TWELVE

Resurrection

The sixth day after the typhoon began with the sky clear and the ocean calm. In every direction, as far as I could see we were surrounded by water. During the night, at a point in time that none of us knew, both Ash and Casleton had slipped away for the last time. There were now just four of us left on the remnant of the raft: Hetzer, Harrison, Hicks, and myself.

We assumed that Ash had swum to our ship resting on the bottom as he had told us so often. In his search for it he must have become separated from the raft to the extent that he was unable to find his way back. Casleton had likely failed to return from one of his extended attempts to locate the ship tender.

Ash's wife had come out from Connecticut to visit her husband when we had been berthed at San Pedro. I had arranged a private dinner aboard the ship for them along with Harrison and his wife. Both Harrison and Ash had joined me for golf the previous Christmas day, just before we were transferred to New York.

Harrison and I had every reason to be deeply distressed at Ash's loss. I'm certain Hicks and Hetzer had also known him well. All of us had known and liked the gregarious, fun-loving Casleton. Yet, sitting there on that balsa wood rim, not one of us displayed or voiced the slightest reaction. I don't believe we had any emotional response at all. We were numb, no longer capable of a human reaction to tragedy and loss.

In fact, *all* emotional response was now absent within us. In other circumstances, the deaths of Ash and Casleton would have moved us profoundly. But floating like this, hours away from our own deaths, beaten by the elements and deprived of all nourishment, emotion of any kind had been discarded as a luxury. Our bodies had begun to feed on themselves, and our life fluids were now reduced to their most critical and dangerous point. Why feel sorry at the loss of friends when we would so soon join them? If there was any emotional capacity within us, it was reserved for pity—pity for ourselves and our increasingly certain end.

The sun shown more brilliantly than on any day since we were cast adrift. Not long after sunrise we detected a distant island partially obscured by the light morning haze. We speculated briefly as to which island it might be but soon abandoned the effort of talk. What difference did it make? It was too far away to offer any hope. We were too exhausted to even consider making an attempt for it. Even more significantly, our mental drive was gone. We had given up. Within the hour the island was no longer visible.

Surviving the previous night had been all that I could bear. I was no longer experiencing feelings of frustration or despair, but I also did not possess the slightest hope. I was beyond emotions, beyond caring. Some part of me, a measure of each of us, understood that we were not far from death, yet I recall experiencing no fear at the prospect. Although I clung to life, in many ways death offered a release from my misery. There was no choice for any of us other than to accept the finality of our circumstance.

Having survived the war, our approaching death was not something that any of us considered normal. Each of us had understood that our death during war was possible. With its ending, we had thought that prospect gone. No violence awaited us now, other than a shark attack or another storm. What stood before us was an entirely different ending. Every hour that passed without food, and especially without water, meant that our life was gradually ebbing away.

In a very detached manner my thoughts turned abstractly to my increasingly distant family. I was no longer worried about not being there for them or of the difficulties they would endure because of my absence. It seemed as if every part of me—physical, emotional, and spiritual—was synchronized to come to a merciful end at the same moment.

There was almost no conversation as we slowly drifted in the water. We were resigned to our deaths and our minds no longer commanded false hopes in the form of fantasies.

The day passed in numbing lassitude. I had lived more than one lifetime since our ship exited Buckner Bay. Even the terror of the typhoon was now a memory so distant that it had no meaning. My universe was here, on this bit of a raft, rocking with the placid movement of that vast ocean. From time to time I fell asleep and toppled into the water, just as the other three did. I know I spent much of the day slipping in and out of a state of lucidity.

I sat motionless and stared ahead with a blank look, my eyes unfocused and devoid of expression. I felt no hope of any kind, no fear of what awaited me. I experienced neither hunger nor thirst. Entire periods of that long day passed without a surviving memory although I know that we all shared the certainty that this was our final day. Not one of us would make it through another night—assuming we survived the day. We were deadened to our fate and sat there accepting whatever was going to happen.

All of us had prayed these past days. Today was no different. We prayed within ourselves and we prayed aloud individually. For the first time, the four of us prayed together. Our prayers were from our childhood, with slightly different words in some cases because of our various faiths. The prayers and passages came from us without prompting.

Hicks delivered a long and deeply moving prayer. He was a shy young man from the deep south. He did his part aboard ship and had seemed to me to be quite ordinary. I no longer remember Hicks's prayer, but what I do recall is how profoundly it moved me. It was eloquently spoken and obviously heartfelt. The fact that Hicks could utter such a deeply touching prayer in such circumstances completely altered my opinion of him. If our true character is to be found within the depths of adversity, then I have no doubt I glimpsed Hicks's strength. I have no way of knowing, but perhaps that was the moment he discovered his own strength within himself.

At some point I came out of a fantasy and announced, "I just saw the captain." The others stared at me strangely. "I asked him to get us our back rations. He promised he'd see to it for us."

Harrison said quietly, "Elm, you didn't see the captain—not really." The other two agreed. "You only imagined it, Mr. Renner," Hicks said politely.

I realized that I had been the only one to experience a fantasy. It was the only delusion I recall from that day. It was disturbing because it meant I was destined to follow on the downward spiral of Ash, Casleton, and Perry.

Until now, every fantasy had spread to others, yet no one picked up this one. I can't explain it. There was also no more talk of tunnels, tubes, or cruising taxis. No discussions about our ship resting on the ocean floor beneath us. Those delusions had been necessary to us—they were apparently still necessary to me—but as we moved steadily toward our death, fantasies no longer served a group purpose. We were now resigned to our pending demise.

If we had spotted another island, even one quite close, we no longer possessed the will to try to reach it, let alone the physical ability to make the attempt. We had suffered five and a half days and nights without water, without food, and with no sleep of any consequence. We existed in a state of numbing despair.

Swaying gently on the raft we rarely spoke. During periods of alertness each one of us scanned the sky and water out of habit but with no expectation. For a brief time we wondered aloud which of us would die next, but only spoke of it in general speculation. We accepted that it could be any of us, at any moment. Our claim to life had become tenuous in the extreme. Hours passed in stupor with nothing but the gentle rocking of the raft, the lapping of the water, and the expanse of the brilliant blue sky. Shortly after noon, Hicks said, "If I'm the first to die, you can drink my blood and eat my body."

No one raised any objection. That's what we were reduced to: cannibalism. With no regard for our moral or religious beliefs, with no meaningful discussion, each of us solemnly made the same pledge to the others.

That afternoon three navy planes, Corsairs, flew over us at low altitude, much closer than any had previously. We made a feeble attempt to attract their attention but the planes flew on. Without a word we returned to our previous state. No one expressed any disappointment. It was almost as if we didn't care if the planes had spotted us.

The ocean was nearly still. We sat, each of us on his own side of the rim, facing one another in silence. We tumbled into the water at regular intervals, then slowly pulled ourselves out and resumed our places.

It was during this long afternoon that I experienced the most peculiar sensation of the entire ordeal adrift. Not one of us had so much as spoken the names of the three men we had lost the night before. We had by now recognized that they were really gone, but there was no discussion of it. No one expressed remorse or grief. None of us had said a word about their fate. There was also no talk about McQueen who had taken off for the island the day before. We'd seen Talley attacked by a shark and knew how likely it was McQueen had died the same way, but not one of us spoke of him.

At this time the day before we had been eight. We didn't know what had happened to McQueen as he'd tried to swim to the island. Three more of our shipmates had simply vanished into the black ocean. We four were all that remained.

Yet we expressed not the slightest notice of any of the men who were no longer with us, any more than we did for our loved ones at home. Being so utterly without emotion still troubles me deeply. I experience a hollow feeling when I allow myself to remember my lack of feelings that day. I felt nothing at their loss, absolutely nothing. Never before or since have I experienced such an emotional wasteland.

The sun edged toward the horizon. Soon we would be facing another dreadful night. Not one of us believed we would survive it. Each of us looked at the sinking sun from time to time, thought the same thoughts. There was nothing to say. There was nothing we could do.

We saw the three Corsairs coming toward us again, flying at approximately the same altitude as before, going the opposite direction. "Bill," I said to Harrison, "wave your white shorts at them. Maybe they'll see us this time." My mouth was so parched, my tongue so swollen, the words came out thick and slurred.

Harrison rose. I held his slimy legs for support as he waved his white shorts at the fast approaching planes. Each of us watched as the three planes passed overhead then sped away. They had clearly been somewhere and were now on their way back, oblivious to the water below.

When we first spotted the planes earlier that day, a weak wave of hope had passed through us. It had quickly died as we watched the planes fly out of sight. With their unexpected return, and now their departure, we turned our eyes back to the water. No one spoke. No one moved other than Harrison as he resumed his place.

We were resigned once again to the reality that no one had spotted us. I glanced a last time at the retreating planes. At that moment, just as they were about to vanish, one of the three planes peeled away from the other two and made a sharp, 180-degree turn, and flew straight at us. I held my breath as the plane dove even lower.

There could be no doubt. We had been spotted!

As the plane passed directly overhead, the pilot tossed out an inflated rubber raft. This probably was his own emergency supply. We knew it held provisions. The raft struck the water a hundred yards away from us. The Corsair then turned and left. We didn't care where it went or why because we knew beyond doubt that help was coming!

The other two planes flew over us as well, each dropping a fluorescent marker of a livid green stain so anyone sent to find us would have no trouble. Because it was fluorescent we knew we would be spotted even in the dark if we had to wait that long. The planes came overhead again and each pilot tossed out survival gear before flying on.

For all this, the answer to our prayers, our response was subdued. We turned our cracked, swollen lips into fleeting smiles, revealing yellow teeth. We maybe uttered a word or two, but that was it. Our despair and our suffering had been within us, and it was there that we held our excitement.

Slowly, our enthusiasm returned and we stirred from our lethargy. Instantaneously, or so it seemed, our minds cleared. We knew beyond any doubt that we could survive until our rescue. To endure that brief stretch of time was nothing.

Curiously, we made no attempt to retrieve any of the supplies dropped to us. We knew the difficulty of trying to move the raft and we lacked any energy. Someone suggested one of us could swim to a rubber raft but we suddenly remembered that there were certain to be sharks nearby. No one was willing to put himself in danger with rescue so close at hand. We could wait this little bit more.

Before long the first Corsair returned, followed by a much larger plane. A PBM, the so-called flying boat, it was often used for sea rescues because it could land in the water. We realized there was no more waiting, our salvation was at hand. We had survived!

The PBM over-flew us once to take a look. Then it turned, lowered itself as it cut speed, and landed in the water with a gentle splash. With its engines pounding it taxied slowly toward us. The propellers looking frightening as the plane drew close and for a crazy moment I wondered if we would be sliced to pieces. Just then the pilot cut the engines. As the plane drifted by a crewman standing on the wing cast us a line. The plane continued to coast and dragged us the short distance as we were reeled in. Both the raft and plane were bobbing gently in the water. Men on the plane reached out for us.

As I was lifted from the raft my head struck the side of the doorway. I recall thinking for an instant, *I can stand no more*. At that moment I passed out.

In the oblivion of my unconsciousness the PBM raced across the ocean, bouncing a time or two, then bore the four of us aloft, raised from the dead like Lazarus from the tomb.

THIRTEEN

Home

In May 1958 I was traveling in Europe on business and lunched at the Eiffel Tower's restaurant. My wife, Dorothy, had remained at home with our four wonderful daughters.

Following the war, I had returned to work for the Stephens Adamson Manufacturing Company in Aurora, Illinois. At the time of my European trip, my company, in combination with Goodyear Tire and Rubber Company, was attempting to sell the New York Transit Authority a system for moving people between Grand Central Station and Times Square. The chairman of the New York Transit Authority was in Paris. As manager of research and development for Stephens Adamson, I was asked to entertain him for a few days. One of our lunches was at the Eiffel Tower with its stunning view of the surrounding gardens and magnificent city.

Traveling with the chairman was Monsignor G. G. Duggan of St. Andrew's Rectory in New York. While we were placing our orders Father Duggan leafed through notes and apparently came upon a small pamphlet he wanted to share with us. As I was speaking to the chairman, Father Duggan slipped it across the table and placed it beside my plate. I saw that it contained a poem, which I glanced at as the chairman was placing his order. My eyes fell to the word "raft" and I was transfixed. As I slowly read the poem I was dumbfounded and from that day forward, for more than forty years, I have carried that poem with me.

How Powerful Is Prayer
In three small rafts, long miles from land,
They battled sharks on every hand—
And prayed.
Storm swept upon an angry sea
For what seemed an eternity,
They prayed.
When water was denied to them
They pled with him of Bethlehem
For rain.
And answering their tortured pleas
He set their awful thirst at ease.
Fresh water.
. . . burrowed deep inside [part of line missing due to fold in paper]
To him quite unashamed they cried
For food.
And granting graciously their wish
There leaped upon one raft a fish—
Fresh food.
When hope had waned and death was near
They called to him in voices clear

For help.
And harkening unto their cries
Planes dropped from out the tropic skies
With help.
Lives there a man who dares to say
He does not hear us when we pray?

I looked up at Father Duggan with what I'm certain was a very strange expression. I said something—I have no memory what—then immediately wondered if I should tell my story. I decided to mention it in passing, but bit by bit the two men drew the entire account from me. I wept as Father Duggan rose and embraced me with tears in his eyes.

On the day of our rescue, 21 September 1945, I came to consciousness as I was carried aboard the USS *Pine Island*, a navy air-sea rescue ship anchored in Chimu Wan, just north of Buckner Bay. Harrison, Hetzer, Hicks, and I were taken to private beds in sick bay, the modest hospital aboard ship. We received small drinks, no more than three ounces, of grapefruit juice from a half-gallon bottle. We were also given intravenous fluids to reverse our dehydration and the resulting chemical imbalance it was causing. Our bodily fluids would be replenished slowly.

Giving us so little to drink was not the result of cruelty or indifference. Men in our pitiful condition had been known to guzzle liquids, then lapse into shock and die. The U.S. Navy had learned from long experience to move cautiously in such situations. The IV was nourishing our bodies even as our incredible thirst remained.

I was left alone for a few minutes, alone with the nearly full can of juice sitting on the table beside me. I took another small sip. So, so, so good. I took another, then another, each larger than the one before. Before I realized it I had drunk the entire half-gallon can of grapefruit juice. Fortunately, I suffered no ill effects from it. When I saw the other three survivors a bit later I told them I'd guzzled the juice, only thinking of their best interest because I didn't want them having stomach cramps. I guess it was amazing that we could joke at a time like this. Not long after that they were given a great deal more to drink, although I was given nothing more when the empty can was seen.

Later we were each offered a cigarette and each one of us refused. It turned out that not one of us had smoked, putting us in the minority of the navy at the time. Of the original nine men on the raft, we were the only four who did not smoke. As I thought about it I realized something else different about us. We four had also been the most active in the ship's athletic program and may very likely have been the fittest of the crew.

I never had a chance to talk to or thank the pilots who saved our lives. The odds against them spotting us in the water were enormous. I'm deeply grateful that at least one of the pilots took the time to scan the water instead of his instrument panel.

Following my ordeal, my physical condition was very poor although not critical. I was diagnosed with exhaustion from over-exposure and was experiencing marked dehydration. I had lost sixteen pounds, most of it in fluids. I had deep necrotic ulcerations on my legs, buttocks, and hands. My legs were extremely sensitive to any kind of pressure. The ulcers were treated with boric acid. Although they appeared to heal almost at once, I suffered for some time from a deep-seated, severe pain in both legs. I was unable to eat normal-sized meals. For weeks I was fed small servings several times a day. I suffered from acute gas after each meal. It was advised that adequate physical therapy facilities were necessary for treatment. The doctors noted on my chart that I was extremely fatigued, restless, and irritable, so I was ordered to be returned stateside.

The last day aboard the *Pine Island* I went topside to get some fresh air and look over the bay. While standing at the rail I happened to glance at a seasoned sailor standing next to me and noticed the profound difference in the color of our skin. I was, to say the least, a dozen shades darker than the leather-skinned old salt. It was only then that I realized just how dark I was from my prolonged exposure to the sun.

Harrison, Hicks, Hetzer, and I had plenty of time to talk, and that's what we did, almost nonstop. But we spoke very little about what we had just endured or of the loss of our shipmates. Five days after our rescue I was transferred to tent hospital SAH-6 on Okinawa.

When I arrived home in October, I learned that my wife had received a telegram on 26 September, *five days after my rescue.*

> I DEEPLY REGRET TO INFORM YOU THAT YOUR HUSBAND, LIEUTENANT (JG) ELMER JOHN RENNER, USNR IS MISSING AS RESULT OF TYPHOON 16 SEPTEMBER 1945 IN THE SERVICE OF HIS COUNTRY. YOUR GREAT ANXIETY IS APPRECIATED AND YOU WILL BE FURNISHED DETAILS WHEN RECEIVED.
>
> VICE ADMIRAL LOUIS DENFELD THE CHIEF OF NAVAL PERSONNEL

The day after my rescue I wrote Dorothy a letter, telling her I was all right and to disregard any other, conflicting information she might receive from the navy. I wrote a similar letter to my parents. My wife's letter arrived ten days after I was rescued. I don't believe I have ever adequately grasped the pain she suf-

fered during that time. On 4 October, a few hours *after* my letter arrived, she received another telegram.

> I AM PLEASED TO INFORM YOU THAT YOUR HUSBAND LIEU-
> TENANT (JG), ELMER JOHN RENNER, USNR PREVIOUSLY REPORTED
> MISSING AS RESULT OF TYPHOON 16 SEPTEMBER 1945 WHILE IN
> THE SERVICE OF HIS COUNTRY IS NOW REPORTED TO BE A SUR-
> VIVOR. UNDOUBTEDLY HE WILL COMMUNICATE WITH YOU AT AN
> EARLY DATE CONCERNING HIS WELFARE AND WHEREABOUTS. THE
> ANXIETY CAUSED YOU BY THE PREVIOUS MESSAGE IS DEEPLY
> REGRETTED.
>
>   VICE ADMIRAL LOUIS DENFELD THE CHIEF OF NAVAL
> PERSONNEL

The end of World War II did not occur during the Stone Age.
The U.S. Navy had ample experience sending telegrams and dis-
patching word to families throughout the war. By late 1945 they
should have perfected the technique. I find it inexcusable that it
took ten days after the capsizing for the navy to send telegrams
to my wife and parents notifying them that I was missing. I
don't know the reason for the delay, but the telegram made it
seem as if there was no hope for my survival. Even more inexcusable, I had been picked up five days *before* the telegram was
sent. This is compassion? This is competence? I find it down-
right inhumane and cruel.

    The Japanese named our storm the Makurazaki typhoon
because it struck the Makurazaki Cape in southern Japan with
great fury. According to the Japanese Meteorological Agency, sustained winds, which would have been diminished from those we
faced aboard YMS-472 and in our raft, were recorded at 115 miles
per hour on the Japanese islands. The storm destroyed 273,888

homes and killed 2,473 people. Another 1,283 were reported as being lost. Our fate was just part of a greater human tragedy.

Of the hundreds of U.S. ships that had put to sea from Buckner Bay, a total of five were lost in the typhoon: four minesweepers and a small submarine chaser. A total of eighty-nine servicemen died. Over the years I have received many letters from the loved ones of some of those lost aboard other ships, asking for information about the storm and what took place.

Although the U.S. Navy had committed to improving its weather reporting following heavy shipping losses sustained from two typhoons the previous year, little progress had been made by September 1945. Each ship anchored in Buckner Bay received word late. When we were informed of the coming storm, the true urgency of the situation was not adequately conveyed. To reach safety we should have been under way hours earlier instead of wasting precious time securing items or trying to retrieve difficult anchors.

I have since heard some stories of the other ships caught in the typhoon. YMS-183 was racing ahead of the storm, just reaching Okinawa from Saipan as we were clearing the harbor. She was refused permission to enter and ordered to sail up the east coast of the island and on to Unten Ko. Approaching Okinawa from a southerly direction, YMS-183's captain elected to take a course *south* of Okinawa, then up the west coast of the island. This placed Okinawa between YMS-183 and the typhoon, significantly mitigating the force of the wind and especially the waves. She reached the safe anchorage, survived the storm, and picked up two survivors from a small craft.

YMS-421, also just arriving from Saipan, was refused entry and ordered to sail to Unten Ko. Shortly after this communication and right at the entrance to Buckner Bay, she was struck by a massive wave that tore away the bridge and caused the ship to break up. Eight were lost but the rest of the crew survived.

The other three minesweepers with YMS-472 on its passage across the Pacific Ocean from San Pedro to Okinawa survived the typhoon. YMS-292's anchor was caught in a cable so she took some time to clear the harbor. She arrived at the entrance to Unten Ko at 1830 and rode out the storm. YMS-292 returned to Buckner Bay the morning of 18 September. Another typhoon struck Okinawa on 10 October. Although washed aground, YMS-292 again survived. She went on to sweep mines off the Japanese coast and was struck from the U.S. Naval Registry in February 1947.

YMS-436 reached Unten Ko where she survived the storm. She too returned to Buckner Bay on 18 September. She experienced no difficulty with the second typhoon. She also swept for mines off the coast of Japan and was struck from the naval registry in March 1947.

Our companion ship in New York, against whose crew we played basketball so often, YMS-454 also found her anchor fouled on a cable when she attempted to leave the bay the morning of the typhoon. She managed to clear her anchor and reached Unten Ko where she moored alongside YMS-404. She also returned to Buckner Bay on the eighteenth. On 9 October she was caught out to sea when the second typhoon struck. The ship was abandoned and all hands swam ashore safely. The ship was struck from the naval registry in January 1946.

Buckner Bay is located near the southern tip of Okinawa. Plan X-ray, as the plan for moving to Unten Ko in the event of a typhoon was called, directed the ships to move along the side of the island facing the approaching storm. In other words, our orders were to sail where we would be subjected to the full fury of the typhoon. If we had instead gone south and rounded the tip of the island we would have moved up the island toward the safe anchorage with the entire island of Okinawa protecting us from the waves and wind, as happened for YMS-183. Although covering a slightly greater distance and taking more time, this passage would have been much safer because the storm descended so quickly. I learned our squadron commander decided that going around the southern end would have placed us in danger of the shoals at that end of the island as well as placed us in major traffic leaving Naha Bay.

It's really impossible to second-guess the decision to send us by the route we took. At the time the order was given it was not yet certain which side of the island the storm would pass, so I doubt any consideration was given to the longer route. In the end a relatively small percentage of ships and seamen were lost, so I suppose naval officers felt justified that they had made the right decision. The longer route would have subjected more ships to danger for a longer period of time.

In the years since the capsizing of YMS-472 I have struggled to come to terms with what I endured and did, or failed to do. I wrote a brief account of the experience for my immediate family because I was asked so often about what happened. Over the years, and especially since my retirement, I continued to research and gather information on the storm itself and the surrounding events.

The U.S. Navy, I learned, constructed 481 YMS minesweepers during the war. A total of thirty-two were lost, sixteen from enemy action and the others due to weather and sea conditions. YMS-472 and three others foundered off Okinawa during the Makurazaki typhoon. When another typhoon struck three weeks later, drawing no doubt on our experience, four minesweepers of the YMS class were beached by their captains rather than risk facing the storm on the open sea. Three ships of the class that elected to ride out the storm capsized.

When the original nine of us had survived the capsizing and the typhoon, we had been extraordinarily unlucky in nearly every regard. From the point of our sinking, which was some twenty to twenty-five miles east of the northern tip of Okinawa, we drifted in a generally northern direction. On the afternoon of the day following our capsizing, the tug ATA-188 discovered two bodies and one survivor from our ship. We then drifted on a northwesterly course, taking us past Okina-Erabu Shima. On 19 September Talley was killed by sharks attempting to reach what we thought was Okinawa. McQueen had swum toward what we thought was Iheya Shima. By the time of our rescue on 21 September we were some ten miles north of Tokuno. Our drift was taking us far from any land, into the barren regions of the East China Sea. Later we learned that both Talley and McQueen swam toward the island of Tokuno Shima.

I have no satisfactory explanation as to why the ships anchored in Buckner Bay received so little information. I don't know what the command of the fleet knew about the storm but I am certain they knew more than "the storm is coming from the south," the only information we received aboard YMS-472. We received not another signal, not one update, absolutely nothing. We were left in the dark and as a result had no information on which to base any decisions. The decisions we made in the end were nothing more than guess work. The most basic information such as the location of the eye of the typhoon, surface speed, and direction could very well have saved us as well as the other ships and crews that were lost.

But this would not necessarily have been the case. Jim Carrier's *The Ship and the Storm*, published by International

Marine/McGraw Hill in 2001, recounts the fate of the cruise sailing ship *Fantome* when it attempted to ride out Hurricane Mitch in 1998. The vessel was nearly three hundred feet long with a crew of forty-five. Originally constructed of wood, her hull was later covered with steel. Equipped with the latest communications and navigation gear, throughout her struggle her captain and crew were in constant contact with shore so they received the most current information on the hurricane. No matter which course the captain set to avoid the storm, Mitch moved relentlessly toward the ship, almost as if it was stalking it. *Fantome* was lost with all hands.

It has taken me decades to finally accept the fact that no meaningful search was ever conducted for us. I believe that never before in the history of mankind have greater resources been available for such a search, resources that had no other mission. As we vainly scanned the sky for planes, air crews passed their days writing letters, trying to fill the tedious hours until they were rotated home. Planes remained on the ground in peak flying condition. A mountain of aviation fuel meant for the invasion of Japan remained in storage, unused. An entire fleet of navy ships was available. Even after ATA-188 made its discovery of two bodies and one survivor, she made no additional searches. Only four YMSs were sent to search the area where the tug had made its recovery. The YMSs spent less than a half day searching before they were ordered back to Buckner Bay. That was the extent of the search for us. Those of us who survived the typhoon were simply written off. Worse, the ships returning from Unten Ko were advised that there were *no* survivors.

I have no explanation other than to believe that a certain callousness had crept into commanding officers' thinking because of the heavy losses suffered during the war. Drifting at sea each of us had feared again and again that we had been written off. We were right.

While I was in the tent hospital another typhoon struck Okinawa. I was certain I would be blown away along with the entire hospital. Highly agitated, I was strongly sedated and moved into the basement of a cement building where I sat out the storm without incident.

Harrison, Hetzer, and Hicks weren't so lucky. They were still aboard a ship, an LST, when the second storm struck. I learned that when she was ordered out to sea they panicked. They begged the captain to beach the ship or at the least allow them to jump overboard while they were still in Buckner Bay. When the captain refused both requests they rushed to the galley and strapped provisions to their bodies. They were forced to ride out the storm aboard the ship.

In October 1945 I was transferred to a hospital in Hawaii. I began the painful process of coming to terms with the full extent of the losses. I was overwhelmed with grief at the deaths of so many friends, so many wonderful young men. Their lives should still have been ahead of them. I have to this day never fully recovered from that grief.

I had a great deal of difficulty sleeping. While in Hawaii I awakened from one nightmare screaming. I had been back in the typhoon during that first horrible, endless night. Having roused most of the other patients, I could hardly look them in the eye the next morning because I was so ashamed.

Although it was the worst nightmare I ever experienced, others continued for many years before finally fading away. My nightmares were always about the first terrifying night on the raft, fighting the waves and wind. As I have written these words, revisited the memories, the nightmares returned intermittently.

Like nearly everyone who served during World War II, I received no counseling. There would not have been enough counselors to help every veteran who had suffered traumatic experiences. It was a different time, a different generation. You were expected to bear difficulties without complaint, without trying to elicit sympathy.

I am unable to discuss, or write, of these events for more than a few short minutes without breaking into tears. I cannot watch a television show with a violent sea scene without, at the least, becoming melancholy.

In May 1994 I read an article in *Reader's Digest* about a woman who had survived the sinking of her ship. Her book was called *Albatross*. After anguishing about my choices, I contacted the author, Deborah Scaling Kiley, through her publisher. We spoke by telephone and shared our mutual experiences. I excerpted a short portion of her text from the magazine and mounted it on my desk. It reads:

> I rarely talked about what had happened to me that October. I never told anyone, not even my husband, about the sheer terror. I thought that if I did normal things like getting married and have babies, then I would be normal too. But I was wrong. Things got better only when I began to reveal what had occurred. And, in the end, telling the story saved my life.

Although I did not understand her advice at the time, I believe this event was a crossroads for me. In time it led to my telling my story here.

After convalescing for a short time in Hawaii I was transferred to San Francisco. I then traveled by train to a hospital in New York state. The route took me through Chicago and I enjoyed a two-day layover with my family. My wife, dad, and brother met me at the train station. I recall that in the moments before stepping from the car I paused to compose myself, wiping tears from my eyes. Questions from my loved ones were almost exclusively concerning my health. I believe this was a result of a natural hesitation to have me relive my experiences.

In mid-January 1946, I was released from the hospital in New York and was ordered to Washington, D.C. As the only surviving officer of YMS-472 it was now my painful duty to file a complete report. I also had to write letters to the families of my shipmates whose fate was still unknown. Assigned to the Bureau of Naval Personnel, I dealt with the dozens of unresolved questions, one of which was whether the men not known to be survivors should be listed as dead or listed as missing. I advised changing their status to dead.

I provided many details of my own experience in my report for the navy. I slowly learned more about what had happened. I learned that the tug ATA-188 pulled George Wade from the sea, wearing just his life jacket. This obviously was when we saw the ship turn away from us on the raft on 17 September. I also learned that just prior to finding Wade, the tug had recovered the bodies of Bob Hobart and John Foster. After making this discovery and entering an obvious debris field of the sunken YMS-472, the tug made no further search in the area but continued on her course.

Shockingly, I learned that Niles McQueen was not dead. He had made it to the island! I only recently found out that initially he told no one that seven of us were still out there on the raft. Later he did reveal that others remained on the raft, but it was too late for the three we lost that night. I can't help but feel that he left us to die. Some two years after our rescue, I had an occasion to speak with him for just a few minutes. He told me that when he reached shore he gave his life jacket to someone as a souvenir. When I asked why he'd done nothing to send help, he claimed that he had passed out immediately after giving away his life jacket. I didn't bother asking him anything else because I remembered that he had always been self-serving. I felt pretty certain that I knew why he'd told no one about us. I didn't press him for details because I feared what I would do if I heard any self-serving lies. I did not think I would be able to refrain from assaulting him.

That McQueen had reached the island and sent no help still deeply disturbs me. Some years later I was visiting with Bill Harrison in California and asked him why he thought McQueen had told no one about us. Bill shrugged and said, "I felt he wanted to be the only survivor of the 472." That's what I think as well. He had simply abandoned us to die.

Harrison told me something I did not know. Shortly after McQueen's rescue, his mother called Bill's wife to express her condolences because Bill had not survived aboard the raft. We talked about it and decided the only reason for this call was because McQueen had told his mother he was the only survivor.

McQueen's marriage didn't last after the war. He died in 1985 of complications from diabetes. When I tried to learn a bit more about him, his son told me he had never really known his father. He asked me not to speak to his mom as she was in very poor health.

I have had many years to consider McQueen's behavior and my opinion of him. For a fact I know that when he landed on the island he had the means to get immediate help to us. Over the years I have tried to think of every imaginable condition that may have influenced his actions when he reached shore that day. Could he have been more delusional than anyone realized? Is it possible that his swim to shore made him even more delusional? Is it possible that by the time he reached shore, he really and truly believed he was the only survivor? Is it possible that the swim made him so demented that he believed everyone else was dead? By the time he came back to the world of the living, is it possible he may have wondered if everyone else was dead, as he believed while he was delirious? Is it possible that he may have felt great shame and remorse?

These questions and others have, at one time or another, floated through my mind. However, each time I conjure up one of these scenarios, none seem to jive with my impression after our conversation in 1947. Although I am firmly of the opinion that he left the seven of us to die, that is something I don't know with absolute certainty. That's as fair as I can be to his memory because what he failed to promptly do upon arriving on land still bothers me.

I was in Washington ten days. I performed my duties in the false belief that the families already knew some details of what had taken place. As a result, my letters were far more cursory, and much less personal, than they should have been, but I didn't know that for many years. The only notification they had received was the official telegram advising that their loved one was "missing." Despite the tremendous resources available to the U.S. Navy, my letter was the first, and only, communication the families of each shipmate received informing them that their loved one was dead.

Over the years these letters have tortured me. Someone more able, more senior than me, should have written them.

Was this minimal effort all a life was worth? Following is a letter, typical of what I wrote:

Dear Mr. and Mrs. Byron,

It is with deepest sorrow that I, as senior survivor of USS YMS-472, write to you concerning the loss of your son, Ralph Byron, who, following the capsizing and sinking of that vessel on 16 September 1945, was listed as missing at sea.

The circumstances surrounding the disaster in which his life was lost are as follows. We were at anchor in Buckner Bay at Okinawa on the Sunday morning of 16 September. At about six o'clock we received word of the approaching typhoon and were told to proceed to an anchorage on the northern tip of the island. We proceeded out of the bay with a group of other small craft, but by noon the seas were mountainous and the vicious typhoon was striking us with all of its violence. We had lost all contact with the other ships now and had decided that it would be best to try and ride the storm out. The tremendous waves were beating us unmercifully with water washing over the entire ship, however, the ship took all this very nicely until about one o'clock the morning of the 17th. Then without any warning, the ship, unable to combat the seas any longer, rolled over on her side, trapping most all of the men that were in enclosures such as the radio room, chart room, and pilot house. Only a few of us were fortunate enough to free ourselves from these enclosures before the ship was completely under water and we took to a life raft. We were at the mercy of the seas for six days before being picked up.

At the time of the capsizing, Ralph was in the pilot-house and it is presumed that he lost his life going down with his ship.

In conclusion, I wish to express my sincerest sympathy to you in your great loss. I hope that the knowledge of your son's splendid service and devotion to duty will give you some measure of comfort and courage. The facts I have told you are complete to the best of my knowledge but if there are any further questions, please do not hesitate to write me in care of the Bureau of Naval Personnel, Navy Department, Room 4040, Washington 25, D.C.

Sincerely yours,

E. J. Renner

Lt. (jg) USNR

Former Engineering Officer

USS YMS-472

All the letters were difficult to write, but the most difficult one was the one I wrote to Boyd Stauffer's wife, Betty. I had met her several times. In fact my wife and I had spent much of the evening at the ship's dance in New York with the Stauffers. I could only imagine how terrible his death had been for her. They had a young son and I wrote him a letter to read when he was grown. Later, I visited with the two of them for a day.

In considering what befell us, I have often thought how the experience of YMS-472 differed from the ships that survived the Makurazaki typhoon. I believe that the 73-degree roll in the end was what sealed our fate. Other ships of our class did not sustain such rolls so their officers were not faced with the same decision that was forced upon us. Other ships continued to the safe harbor and survived. I believe our roll was caused by the convergence of two or more waves and it was our misfortune to sustain the blow from one at a time when other ships did not. It caused us to take a different course of action. I always remember that my ship was not the only minesweeper to capsize in the storm.

Anything I do today is all second-guessing. We did what we believed was necessary then, and it was, tragically, the wrong decision.

I never spoke to my wife, Dorothy, about what happened. I never told the story to others except in the most extraordinary circumstances and then only in a highly abbreviated form. This aversion to speak of the tragedies of the war is one I shared with many veterans. Everyone in my family knew my ship had capsized and that I had drifted for days in a raft, but they knew neither the details nor the full magnitude of the experience. To the extent I could, I concealed from my loved ones the marks the events had seared within me. It was not until 1986 when my oldest grandchild, then eleven years old, asked me about what happened to me in the war that I first came to terms with relating the tragedy.

I wrote, with the help of my son-in-law Steve Burrows, an abridged account of what occurred. Titled *Survival*, I had two hundred copies printed. I distributed them to family and friends. And there the story remained until I retired. As is also true for many veterans, when I retired my thoughts turned back to the war, to the fine young men I had known and the fate we had suffered. I resolved to write a detailed account of the brief life of YMS-472 and her crew.

Because my wife and I had not discussed my ordeal, we also had not discussed what had happened back home. Only in the final stages of writing this book did I learn her story. Dorothy relates:

The last time I had seen my husband, Elmer, was when I visited him in New York to attend the USO-sponsored ship's party. We had a very good time and I had the opportunity to meet and visit with many of his shipmates. I had met a few of them before when I was in Florida while the ship was in construction; however, meeting them at the party was different. It was more relaxed and everyone was in a festive mood. I thought then what a wonderful group of young men. I did look at them and couldn't help thinking that some of them may not come back. Never did I think that the one that may not come back would be my husband.

I knew the ship was going to the Pacific and that Elmer was going to be overseas for a prolonged period of time. The war in Europe was ending, but who knew how long the other conflict would last? We spent several days together. I remember we stayed at the parson's home of a Presbyterian church in Brighton, Staten Island. Elmer had too much to drink at the party. He got sick on the ferryboat and I had to walk him home. The next day I accompanied him to the dock where the ship was tied up at the pier and went aboard. Not being a seafaring person I promptly got seasick. The next day I would be returning to Chicago by train. We said our passionate good-byes.

While Elmer was sailing to the Pacific and on to Okinawa I received letters from him on a regular basis. At the time, even though we had been married for almost two years, we had no permanent place of residence. Like many wives of servicemen, I was staying with my parents. They had a small lower flat with two bedrooms in Aurora. My father was a fireman and living with us was my maternal grandmother, my sister, and our daughter, Patty. It was four generations in one small flat. We were crowded, but that was not unusual in those days.

As a fireman my father worked twenty-four hours on and twenty-four hours off. Given our living conditions, I think he was glad to go to work. My mother was handicapped and my sister was working, so most of the housework fell on my shoulders.

What with taking care of Patty and the household chores, my time was filled. Patty was some fifteen months old and had a habit of crying when being put to bed. If my father was off duty that day, he had a difficult time putting up with a crying baby and would frequently leave the house at Patty's bedtime.

On this Wednesday, we had already had dinner, and in the early evening my father had left the house. The war was over and there was no longer the apprehension that we experienced when it was still raging. September 26th was a beautiful and temperate day. I had Patty out for a walk and we played in the schoolyard across the street from our flat. There were several small pieces of equipment that Patty used to slide on and we frequently played there. It was the grade school I attended when I was a child.

She was tired that day and at about 7:30, just before dusk, I was putting her to bed when the doorbell rang. My sister was home and answered it. She came into the bedroom where I was putting Patty to bed and handed me a telegram. This was completely unexpected and out of the blue. I opened the envelope, expecting possibly some good news about Elmer's anticipated return. I read the first three words, "We deeply regret." I thought, *How can this be? The war was over.* I don't know how to express the impact of those three words, I just don't know how. I didn't faint, but I sat down on the bed, holding the telegram lightly in my hand.

After a few minutes I regained my composure enough to read the entire message. Then we all tried to analyze it. It didn't say much, but what did stand out was that the typhoon was listed as taking place on September 16th. This was the 26th. That was ten long days and we quickly assumed the worst. There was no chance of surviving a typhoon at sea for that long a time. We assumed Elmer was washed overboard because the message did not say the ship was lost.

After a short while I called Elmer's mother and father who had not yet received a telegram. However, as I was talking to them they too had a messenger at the front door with the same telegram. Of course, they were devastated, as were we all. This was the second time my family was exposed to such a message. My sister had been engaged to her boyfriend who had lived in the neighborhood. He was in the Army Air Force and his parents had received a similar telegram the previous year informing them of his death.

How can I explain the horror of receiving a message of that kind without the emotional reaction of pure panic? I went back to the bedroom and looked at Patty. She was asleep by now. I thought, What's in store for us now? What do we do? Where do we go? How do we cope? Questions with no answers.

The next day a reporter from the local newspaper came and wanted a story. We merely handed him the telegram because that was all we knew. There were articles in the local as well as all the Chicago papers. In no time, I began receiving telephone calls from friends and others I didn't even know. Days later letters poured in from all my friends as well as Elmer's. We all assumed the worst with the exception of one.

A letter arrived from a professor at the University of Illinois, Dr. Elhardt. Elmer had worked with him while attending school there. He was a World War I veteran who had his shoulder shot off as well as three of his fingers on his right hand. He wrote a very optimistic letter that gave me some hope, but I knew too much time had passed and it was too late. I knew it, but yet maybe!!!

Elmer's mother was optimistic too. She just knew he would return. His father, on the other hand, was the most pessimistic, constantly repeating, "How can anyone survive a typhoon for this long a time? It's impossible."

The local chapter of the Red Cross called and wanted to assist me in making application for the ten thousand dollar insurance that each serviceman had. However, on rereading the telegram it only said, "missing." To apply it had to say, "presumed dead." They would call back later. I had fully accepted the worst and was doing my best to cope.

On Thursday the 4th of October I was in the backyard playing with Patty when the postman delivered a letter. My mother had it in her hand as she called to me from the back door. She had pondered even giving it too me. She thought it was the last letter Elmer had written before the storm and was late in delivery, not at all unusual. We had all heard such stories. However, she did call me.

I hesitated opening it but I finally did. The very first line began, "Whatever you may have heard about me, I'm OK," and I realized Elmer had been saved. I couldn't contain myself. I picked Patty up and ran into the house. I called Elmer's parents. You could hear the excitement over the telephone. They had not as yet received Elmer's letter to them. Shortly after, they called saying they too received a letter with the good news. Later that evening I received the second telegram from the navy telling of his survival.

What more is there to say?

Over the years I maintained contact with Bill Harrison but before 1986 we rarely spoke of the war and what we had suffered together. We preferred to play golf and remember the good times. As is always the case in situations such as this, Bill's memories in some particulars, while remarkably identical to my own in nearly every regard, do differ. Unlike me, he has often spoken to groups about his experience. He tells how, during that last horrible day, he offered a prayer of thanks to God for our salvation *before* the planes that spotted us had flown over. He believes this with all his heart. I don't doubt his word, but because of my debilitated condition I have no memory of it.

Bill remained a religious man after the war. In fact, being a contractor, I think he built most of the churches in southern California. We still talk from time to time although I don't see him very often anymore.

I lost contact with Bob Hicks. Late one night I received a telephone call from a man who had been drinking. It was Bob, wanting to say hello. We talked and talked, laughed and laughed, until my side hurt. Only after I hung up did I realize I had forgotten to get his address. A few minutes later he called back. Same thing. We talked and talked, laughed and laughed, and once again I forgot to get his address. Although I tried many times since, I was not able to locate him. With deep regret, I finally learned that he died in April 1990. At about the same time I discovered that George Wade had passed away shortly before Christmas 1963. Regretfully, I lost all contact with Freeman Hetzer and every attempt to locate him has proven unsuccessful.

Since that day I was plucked from the Pacific I have lived my life in anticipation that one more terrible event would happen to me. This is, I understand, common to survivors. Several times, I have believed the event to be imminent. Once I was about to board an airplane when I saw that it was flight 472. I fled in panic and tore up the ticket. After sitting in the waiting room to compose myself I went to another airline and caught a different flight.

I've been blessed with the good life I dreamed about during the war. I even indulge in an occasional Black Cow. I have a loving wife and four marvelous daughters with wonderful sons-in-law and families. My rewarding career included thirteen patents, yes, the number is thirteen. When you pick up your luggage at the airport, notice the conveyer belt as it turns a corner. I also played a major role in developing moving walkways as well. Outwardly, I believe I have largely been the man I would have been even if YMS-472 had not capsized. Inwardly I am, in many ways, someone else.

With the coming of summer and especially now during my retirement, I return with my family to our beach house beside Lake Michigan. For all these many years, through the passing of more than half a century, it has been so. My thoughts at dusk when I sit alone on the roof deck of the beach house and gaze across the placid water have remained unaltered by the years. It is as if some part of me has remained behind, suspended still in September 1945. Although the coming of night there beside the water no longer holds me in terror, at such moments it still troubles me deeply.

As the last of light fades from the leaves of the poplar trees and night finally descends in fullness, I enter the main house, to the loving embrace of my wife and the warmth of my family and friends. My thoughts, however, are far away. They remain on those final days of my youth when I was at the mercy of that terrible storm and then adrift in the vast Pacific. I remember when all hope was lost and cherish the memories of the wonderful crew of YMS-472 who died such tragic deaths, so far from home, so very long ago. It is to them I dedicated this book.

FOURTEEN

The Inquiry

Since I began writing this full-length story of my experiences, I simultaneously conducted a comprehensive search of many records, some well known and others only slowly discovered. Thankfully, the Internet opened up many sources to me. After much disappointment I ultimately, and only recently, made contact with two extremely cooperative employees, one at the National Archives and Records Administration in College Park, Maryland, and the other at the Office of the Judge Advocate General of the U.S. Navy at Washington Navy Yard in Washington, D.C. Detailed information has been found in ship logs and war diaries. I gained much knowledge after the first draft of this book was written in the 1990s.

I have also had the pleasure of speaking to and visiting with many men who served on other small YMS minesweepers. Most of them experienced the same storm of 16 September 1945 as I did, so I learned a great deal from our meetings and conversations. With their help and assistance, along with the cooperation of the government employees, I was able to piece together what I now believe to be the greater truth of what really happened during the Makurazaki typhoon and its immediate aftermath.

Understandably, the events of this story have remained very clear in my mind, but I have long sought the answers to nagging questions:

Why was the notice to evacuate Buckner Bay given so late?
What factors contributed to the capsizing of the ship?
What search efforts were made to find survivors of YMS-472?
Who spotted us on the raft? Why was this group of planes flying in the area?
Did McQueen really remain silent about other survivors on the raft after he reached shore?

The last question is the most important. My continuing search for answers has been enlightening.

A U.S. Navy Court of Inquiry into the capsizing and sinking of YMS-472 was held onboard U.S. Coast Guard cutter *Bibb* from 24 September through 2 October 1945, not long after the storm. Given human nature, it is important to remember that those responsible for the decisions leading to loss of life would have been interested in presenting their actions in the best possible light. I was not called to testify. Neither was Harrison, Hicks, nor Hetzer. We were all in the hospital at the time of the inquiry. However, I did obtain a transcript of the inquiry from the Office of the Judge Advocate General of the U.S. Navy.

The following conclusions are drawn from the testimony at the Court of Inquiry; through the logs of many ships, war diaries,

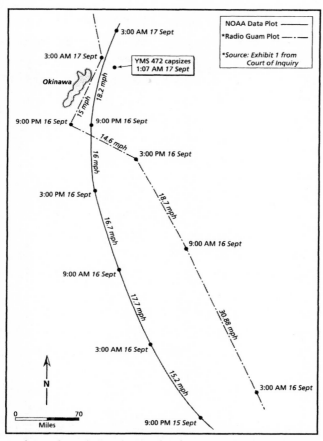

Makurazaki typhoon plotting data by naval aerographer, who
based his coordinates on Radio Guam reports, and National
Oceanic and Atmospheric Administration's (NOAA) plotting
data, 15–17 September 1945.

and weather data; and from the many interviews with members of crews of other ships involved in the storm.

Why was the notice to evacuate Buckner Bay given so late? Lt. Edward Rogers, USNR, was the aerographer from the staff of the Commander of Minecraft Pacific Fleet. He testified at the Court of Inquiry that he recorded and plotted weather and storm information as reported by Radio Guam, which indicated the storm would pass south of Okinawa. The decision to evacuate Buckner Bay on 16 September 1945 was based on that information. The National Oceanic and Atmospheric Administration (NOAA) information for the same period of time and for the same storm differs substantially from Radio Guam. It shows the storm progressing in a steady, broad-sweeping, smooth curve heading directly up the east coast of Okinawa. I believe the late decision to evacuate Buckner Bay was based either on erroneous information given by Radio Guam or the data received from Radio Guam was misinterpreted by the aerographer.

What factors contributed to the capsizing of the ship? Immediately before we capsized I felt the sluggishness of the bow in recovering from each wave. As I was heading for the flying bridge to inform the captain of what I felt, the ship rolled over. The major waves we were encountering were coming from starboard. If YMS-472 had capsized as a result of taking a wave, she would have capsized to port. Our capsizing was to starboard, thus suggesting that something other than taking a wave was responsible.

Both Wade and McQueen were questioned at the inquiry: "Did the ship have an acoustic boom?" and "Was there sluggishness in recovering from the waves before it capsized?" While I had always suspected the pivot joint of the boom to the ship's hull was a probable point of failure, reading the questioning done by the inquiry panel convinced me that a failure had occurred at that joint. I believe the panel also thought the same.

If we had not experienced that near-deadly roll we would not have abandoned our efforts to reach Unten Ko. Turning into the storm, thus striking the waves head-on for a prolonged time, caused the failure of the boom-hull pivot joint. This failure created a flooding of the forward compartments of the ship, destabilizing her buoyancy and leading to our capsizing.

What search efforts were made to find survivors of YMS-472? The Court of Inquiry also solicited testimony about efforts to search for us. Again, remember that men who had a right to expect rescue died even though ample resources existed to search for them. Those responsible for such an effort of necessity were interested in making the best presentation they could. For some, our survival was an embarrassment. It also appears the inquiry panel was not interested in pursuing the matter.

In the questioning of officers from Commander of Minecraft Pacific Fleet, testimony was given that there were five separate operations ordered and conducted to locate and rescue survivors of YMS-472. Tug ATA-188 was sent to search for survivors of YMS-472 while on a mission to provide assistance to USS *Shellbark* (AN-67). The tug's logs indicate otherwise. By accident, on its course to service *Shellbark*, two bodies and one survivor of YMS-472 were discovered and retrieved. Immediately after the recovery, *within minutes*, the tug returned to her base course. There is no mention in her logs of her being sent to search, or that she did search, for survivors of YMS-472. The tug did radio Commander of Minecraft Pacific Fleet the location of her discovery. After ATA-188 completed her mission the next morning, she returned to Buckner Bay. Although she passed

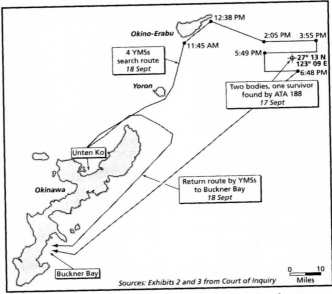

Route taken by four YMSs searching for survivors and route
taken by other YMSs returning from Unten Ko to Buckner
Bay after Makurazaki typhoon.

close by where she had made the initial discovery, the records
do not mention looking for survivors.

The ship that we saw our first day on the raft was heading
directly at us, but she stopped and turned in another direction.
We had seen ATA-188. Why she didn't search in the immediate area for others I'll never know, but I do question the captain's decision to *not search*. He had to know that if he found
three from YMS-472, there probably would be others in the
immediate area. ATA-188 had the best opportunity to find survivors. She was in the *exact* location of the debris field only fourteen or fifteen hours after our capsizing. The debris field was

more than likely still concentrated. ATA-188's discovery of three of my shipmates was shear accident.

The second search operation consisted of four YMS minesweepers sent to the area after the tug's discovery. At first light on 18 September four YMSs were under way to search for survivors of YMS-472. They arrived at the site at 1405. At 1848, after less than five hours of searching the area, they were ordered to discontinue their search and return to Buckner Bay. We saw the four ships only a few miles away. We watched them make their first pass to the south of us sailing east. According to the exhibit at the inquiry, their next two passes were even farther to the south and out of our sight. Because our natural and normal drift was to the north, just why they searched the area south of the identified location as reported by ATA-188 is beyond explanation. But that is exactly what they did.

The fleet of YMSs at Unten Ko was ordered to be on sharp lookout for survivors on its return route to Buckner Bay. The ships left Unten Ko on the morning of 18 September. Their return route would carry them around the northern tip of Okinawa and then south-southwest to Buckner Bay. The location of YMS-472's debris field, as reported by ATA-188, was already known by Commander of Minecraft Pacific Fleet. It was north-northeast, some sixty to seventy miles from the returning fleet's route. In addition, the drift of the debris field was in a northerly direction, further distancing itself from the path of the returning YMSs.

In a later conversation with an officer aboard one of the returning ships I was told that he remembered being told, prior to their return, that there were no survivors from YMS-472. There is no way the returning YMSs could be taken as a search for survivors of YMS-472.

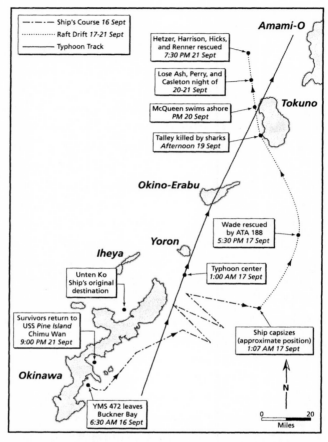

YMS-472's course, raft drift, and Makurazaki typhoon track.

A separate search by a fleet of destroyer minesweepers
(DMSs) of Task Group 52.2 was ordered according to testimony
at the Court of Inquiry. In a review of the logs of USS *Gherardt*
(DMS-30), the command ship of TG 52.2, there is no mention
of a search for survivors of YMS-472. The log does mention
that on 19 September the ship conducted a search for survivors

of YMS-98. The position from which that search was conducted was about one hundred and fifty miles north of the location of YMS-472's debris field.

A review of the war diary of Minecraft Divison 60, also designated as part of TG 52.2, indicated that the only search conducted by TG 52.2 was on 19 September. Searching for survivors of YMS-98, the division task group discontinued its search at 1615 on 19 September. No records indicate that any search was ever made by TG 52.2 for survivors of YMS-472.

According to testimony at the Court of Inquiry, Fleet Air Wing One conducted a search for survivors of YMS-472. In a review of Fleet Air Wing One's war diary for the entire month of September, no mention of a search for survivors of YMS-472 was found. The diary, however, does mention conducting searches for ships in distress around the *southern* shores of Okinawa. YMS-472's debris field, as discovered by ATA-188, was *north and east* of the northern tip of Okinawa. No official records have been unearthed to indicate that Fleet Air Wing One ever searched for YMS-472 survivors.

The only documented search was the search conducted on 18 September by the four minesweepers. They did search the area identified by the tug on the previous day. However, the search lasted for less than five hours before being called off.

Were the lives of thirty-one men worth only a total of five hours of searching? Apparently so!

Who spotted us on the raft? Why was this group of planes flying in the area? This question remains unanswered and I suspect will always remain that way unless I get very, very lucky. I simply have no information about who spotted us. Marine aviators flying Corsair aircraft, probably by shear coincidence, spotted us and sent for assistance from the air-sea rescue ship

USS *Pine Island*. The ship's log shows our being brought aboard at 2100 on 21 September.

Did McQueen really remain silent about other survivors on the raft after he reached shore? Perhaps the most persistent remaining question is establishing whether or not McQueen informed authorities that there were other men still out on a raft. In the Court of Inquiry questioning of McQueen, he reported that at about 1400 on 20 September he swam ashore to Tokuno Shima. He said he was picked up about five hundred yards from shore. Once ashore he was given shoes, trousers, and water. He was then taken to a house where he passed out on the porch. Asked how long it was after he was picked up until he passed out, he testified, "It may have been about twenty minutes." There is no clear indication of who picked him up but it appears he was recovered by natives in the region and then turned over to the Japanese military who in turn gave him to the U.S. military. When the inquiry panel asked McQueen if he had reported there were eight (actually there were seven) men left on the raft, he answered, "No Sir. I passed out." There were no further inquiries as to if or when he finally reported that others remained on the raft.

During my conversation with McQueen in 1947 he stressed the fact that he had passed out immediately after giving his rescuers his life jacket. This obviously was a contradiction of his Court of Inquiry testimony. Furthermore, in his testimony he gave the distinct impression of being sound of mind. He provided specific details of how he reached shore. There was no indication of delusional thinking when he testified in 1945.

In the Court of Inquiry questioning he was asked, "[D]o you know whether an attempt was made to search for them?" His answer was "Not then." However, he must have reported at some time that there were others on the raft because USS *Henry A. Wiley* (DM-29) was sent to search for other survivors of YMS-472 on 22 September. Thankfully, we had already been picked up on the twenty-first. It is doubtful that any of us would have survived the night of 21–22 September on the raft.

There are no questions in the Court of Inquiry testimony that would establish whether or when McQueen told anyone about the men on the raft. In my opinion, even if a communications problem existed, he should have been able to get his message across. In his testimony McQueen said there were fishing boats in the area. At the least, they could have been used to reach us. We had begged him to get help as soon as possible. He had known our condition was critical. *Three men lost their lives that very night!*

My conclusion is that McQueen intentionally made no immediate effort to convey a message to his rescuers about the remaining men on the raft. It is not known when he did tell someone but I suspect it was no earlier than late the following day because it was *two* days later, on 22 September at 1500, that destroyer minesweeper *Wiley* was sent to rescue the survivors from the raft. None of us could have survived that long.

I thought the Court of Inquiry testimony of a few of the officers was obviously directed at obscuring the reality and misleading the panel as to the actual facts regarding the rescue effort. Some of the testimony read like a typical "protect your ass" cover-up. I further thought it inexcusable that the panel made no effort to evaluate or verify the accuracy of the testimony given by the officers.

I find it absolutely incredible that such a callous unconcerned attitude was taken by officials of the U.S. Navy, especially considering that the lives of thirty-one men were at stake. I also find it incomprehensible that the captain of ATA-188 did not make an effort to search the immediate area for additional survivors when he had the best opportunity to do so. If he had found one survivor, there might be others. If nothing else, more bodies might have been recovered. As it was, we were only a few hundred yards away when the tug departed the area.

The information gathered from my research and interviews provided me with many answers to questions I had buried in my mind over the years. I had anticipated more positive results from my investigation of official records. I had always held the U.S. Navy, the branch of the service I had selected, in high regard. But now, after confirming the facts I had only before suspected, I am bitterly disappointed. Knowing the answers to my questions, however, has provided me with a measure of satisfaction and peace of mind. I now know as much as I can ever reasonably expect.

Bibliography

Brady, Ensign Richard, YMS-421, interview with author, 1999.
　　Brady, Richard. "ABC's Life in a Storm." *Chicago Maritime Society Newsletter* 16, no. 1 (winter 2002).

Davis, Ensign John, YMS-183, interview with author, 2003.

Davis, Ensign John Dixon. "Review of Voyage from Saipan to Buckner Bay by USS YMS-183 and others 10–18 September 1945." Unpublished manuscript, 22 May 2001.

Drake Field Okinawa Weather Station, 1945 Makurazaki typhoon data, obtained from the National Oceanic and Atmospheric Administration (NOAA)/National Climatic Data Center, Asheville, North Carolina.

Fleet Air Wing One, War Diary, 1–30 September 1945, National Archives and Records Administration (hereafter NA), College Park, Maryland.

Harrison, Bill, motor machinist mate second class, YMS-472, interviews with author, 2003.

Harrison, Bill. "Bill Harrison Remembers and Is Thankful." *A Look at Whittier* (A Mail Bag publication) 2, no. 9 (November 1954).

Ie Shema Okinawa Weather Station, 1945 Makurazaki typhoon data, obtained from the NOAA/National Climatic Data Center, Asheville, North Carolina.

The Japanese Meteorological Agency, letter from Ryosuke Mizouchi to author's son-in-law Steve Burrows, 28 December 1993.

Jost, Kenneth, chief quartermaster, YMS-421, interview with author, 2003.

Jost, Kenneth. "Last Voyage." Unpublished manuscript, June 1946.

Mine Division 60 (Task Group 52.2) War Diary, 1–30 September 1945, NA.

"Navy Losses in Previous Blow." *New York Times*, 12 October 1945.

Office of the Chief of Naval Operations, Navy Department. *Dictionary of American Naval Fighting Ships*. Volume 5. Washington, D.C.: U.S. Naval History Division, 1970.

Peel, Jim, electrician's mate first class, YMS-421, interview with author, 2001.

Perez, George Sr., seaman first class, YMS-454, interview with author, 2001.

Soukoff, Allan, lieutenant (junior grade), YMS-292, interview with author, 2001.

U.S. Navy, "Record of Proceedings of a Court of Inquiry Convened on Board the U.S.C.G.C. *Bibb* by Order of Commander Minecraft to Inquire into the Circumstances Connected with the Loss of the U.S.S. YMS-472, near Okinawa Shima, on 16 September 1945," 24 September–2 October 1945, transcript, obtained from the Office of the Judge Advocate General of the U.S. Navy, Washington Navy Yard, Washington, D.C. Capt. Leonard Freiburghouse, USN, was the chairman of the Court of Inquiry and Lt. Hamilton Lieb, USNR, was the judge advocate. Also serving were Comdr. Herman T. Diehl, USCG, and Lt. Burton G. Berg, USNR. The following officers testified:

Birdwell, Lt. Donald, USNR, Commanding Officer, YMS-434

Eddy, Comdr. John, USNR, Casualty Officer, Staff of Commander Minecraft Pacific Fleet

Lambert, Lt. Comdr. M. T. Jr., USNR, Commander Mine Squadron 105, ACM-2

Rogers, Lt. Edward, USNR, Aerographer, Staff of Commander Minecraft Pacific Fleet

Smith, Lt. Comdr. Joseph, USN, Medical Officer, Staff of Commander Minecraft Pacific Fleet

Whitemarsh, Capt. Ross, USN, Chief of Staff, Commander Minecraft Pacific Fleet

Wirtz, Capt. Paul, USN, Operations Officer, Staff of Commander Minecraft Pacific Fleet

USS ATA-188, Ship Log, 17 and 18 September 1945, NA.

USS *Dorsey* (DMS-5), Ship Log, 17–20 September 1945, NA.

USS *Gherardi* (DMS-30), Ship Log, 17–19 September 1945, NA.

USS *Henry A. Wiley* (DM-29), Ship Log, 1–30 September 1945, NA.

USS *Pine Island*, Ship Log, 21–29 September 1945, NA.

USS *Planter* (ACM-2), Ship Log, 16–18 September 1945, NA.

USS YMS-292, Ship Log, 16–18 September 1945, NA.

USS YMS-434, Ship Log, 16–18 September 1945, NA.

USS YMS-454, Ship Log, 16–18 September 1945, NA.

USS YMS-472, Ship Log, 11 November 1944–31 August 1945, NA.

About the Authors

Today, Elmer and Dorothy Renner have four children, Patricia, Jane, Sue, and Barbara. They also have six grandchildren, John, Ben Andrew, Jeffrey, Jacey, Jeff, and Callie, and four great-grandchildren.

Co-author Ken Birks died in the spring of 2003. He didn't get to see the final version of this book. His wife, Sylvia, and three children, Barbara, Raymond, and Beverly, and two grandchildren, Kathryn and Anne, survive him.

The fleet of minesweepers that Renner's ship was joining at Okinawa was to sweep for mines in the harbor at Sasebo, a large and important city on the island of Kyushu.

The marine regiment that was to occupy the Sasebo area was the 27th. Birks was a member of that regiment. Renner's fleet was being sent to Japan to clear the harbor of mines for the landing of the 27th Regiment.